MOTHERS OF ANGELS

Inspirational Thoughts for Parents Dealing with Child Loss
Volume One

STEPHANIE BASCO
SULLIVAN

Mothers of Angels
Inspirational Thoughts for Parents Dealing with Child Loss
Volume One

ISBN: 10: 1-888141-24-7
ISBN 13: 978-1-888141-24-5

Published by:
Southeast Media Productions
Carlisle, Pennsylvania
U.S.A.
Semediapro.com

This book is a collection of thoughts and poems written by Stephanie Basco Sullivan. It is based on her posts at the following Facebook page.
For more posts and daily thoughts, please visit
https://www.facebook.com/myheartshapedwomb/

Foreword

I want to share some notes from my book, *Mothers of Angels.*

I have written this book in hopes of bringing awareness to the emotional and physical aspects of losing a child. I wanted to reach out to mothers, fathers and families that have had to endure the horrible tragedy of saying goodbye to their baby or babies, born or unborn. It's the hardest thing I've ever had to do.

I also wanted to let people know the importance of having - and giving - the respect a grieving parent, especially the mother, needs when something like this happens.

That never forgetting the baby - you would have raised - is more crucial than acting as though the tragedy never happened in the first place. I wanted to bring to light the importance of getting help when something like this happens. It's okay to admit defeat in weakness.

You've been through something that will forever change your life. And even though you are a child of God, and you pray and ask God for guidance, it's not a sin to seek help from professionals. It's okay if you are required to take medication every day, several times a day, just to survive.

Life is difficult. Losing a child is the worst thing that some people will ever have to endure.

Don't feel embarrassed, or less of a Christian, if you need extra help getting through the day. Life is unfair, and sometimes, very unforgiving. I don't feel any less connected to God due to my loss. If anything, I feel stronger and more connected to him. I will never know, while I'm still on this earth, why this happened to me. But I know that all will be answered when I see My Lord and Savior.

The good news is that I know where my Makaylee is, and I can't wait to see and hold her. In some ways, I'm grateful that she doesn't have to endure the trials and tribulations of life.

She'll never be sick or broken hearted, and I thank God for that. It doesn't stop me from asking God why, but I'm only human. I'd be lying if I said I've never been angry or I never questioned God.

I hope that my story can help you, or someone you know, get through the loss of a child. If I can help just one mother or father, then I've done what I set out to do.

May God bless and keep you, my dear friend. Know that you are not alone. You are a part of a very unique group of blessed people. You are a mother to an angel, and that's a special honor to hold. A very difficult position, but a special one.

I am a mother to an angel. For over fourteen years now, I have been going to counseling and taking anxiety and antidepressant medications to cope with the mental and physical strain that comes with burying my only child. In reality, we are raised thinking that you're born, live your life, then when your hair turns grey; smooth skin becomes wrinkled and we no longer see or hear like we did in our youth. Death is the next step in the order of things.

But when we hear of, or personally experience, the loss of a child, whether it is in the early stages of pregnancy, weeks, months or shortly after birth, the fragile nature of life becomes very realistic, and we are left with uncertainty and unanswered questions.

And there are not a lot of safe, judgment free zones where bereaved parents can gather from all over the world to come together and unburden their heavy hearts, without anyone making them feel like there's something wrong with them.

One day when I was browsing on social media, I came across a bereaved parent that had bravely shared her story of child loss. Her words rang true in my heart. I felt a pull on my soul that maybe I needed to start a page where mothers and fathers could stand on their soap box despite those who judge them on how they mourn their child. A laid back atmosphere where everyone could relate to one another on how they felt - adjust to the new world they've been forced to live in.

Even if we have a good support system or outlet for our grief, sometimes opening up to others who don't personally know you, but fully empathize with what you are going through, is so much easier, because there is not a one-sided atmosphere. Just everyday people that share one thing in common - the untimely death of their child. So, I created the Facebook page, *Mothers of Angels* (Look for "Mother's of Angel's" at " at https://www.facebook.com/myheartshapedwomb/).

A safe place for parents to talk and share with one another about their heartache, along with keeping the precious memories we have of our children alive, for that is all we have. I'm very blessed to say we are six hundred members strong and counting. I have met some very precious people, friends for a lifetime. A group of people, just like me, that can support each other through the good times and the bad.

My hope is that you find some comfort and encouragement with these poems and messages that I have posted on *Mothers of Angels*. Love and hugs, my friend.

For more posts and daily thoughts, please visit https://www.facebook.com/myheartshapedwomb/:

1

At the end of the day, the most important thing to remember is even though we cannot hug our babies, it doesn't mean that they aren't hugging us.

The pain, that heart wrenching ache that is felt in the pit of our stomachs, is proof that your love is never ending for your angel. The smile that forms on your face after reflecting on a memory is their loving embrace.

2

Love is unconditional. Especially for parents who have lost a child. We have to love our babies from afar and yearn for the day we are reunited with them. We know that God is taking good care of them, but we still long to have that experience for ourselves.

One way we can show and feel the love we wish we could give our angels is by keeping flower arrangements and sentimental trinkets that remind us of them at their place of rest.

I have found this to be very therapeutic, and I feel like I'm not only showing my love for my daughter, but I'm also blessed with some peace of mind, if only for a little while. Love and hugs, my friends.

3

Hello, dear friends. It's perfectly okay to talk about depression and anxiety you have after losing a child - it's only natural. Please don't think that counseling and modern medication makes you weak. If anything, getting the extra help you need to push through the tough times - and those yet to come is - showing your courage and strength. Some people can push aside their feelings and freely judge those of us that can't. But I'm here to tell you, that is not a healthy or safe way to deal with your pain. All that does is leave room for more heartache to build up. Eventually, the weight of your pinned-up grief and anger will wind up causing you to be completely destroyed from the inside out. So, cry when you need to. Visit your child's graveside as often as you like. I often talk to my daughter while I clean her headstone and figurines, and somehow, this makes me feel connected with her as a mother. Love and hugs, my friends.

4

We all have mental and physical scars. These are proof of our living testimony. They also make us unique. Every time I see the scar running up and down my abdomen, I'm reminded that I was going to be a mother, but now it only brings back memories of a life lost and a dream crushed. And now that my beloved four-legged fur baby, Shayla, has gained her wings and joined her sister, my emotional scar on my heart has doubled - but yet, I press forward. We might not like our scars, but in their own way, they are beautiful. Sad reminders, but beautiful memories. Love and hugs, my friends.

5

Envision standing by the banks of a river at sunset. The water slowly trickles by with the push of a soft breeze. As the sun begins to settle on the horizon, the bold, beautiful colors of orange and deep pinks cover the endless sky.

You know, as humans, we don't always understand why we go through the trials and tribulations we face every day. But as I look at a sunset, I am reminded that God has a purpose for everything. He is always in control, even when we feel like he isn't. Everything happens in his timing, and his timing is perfect. I know, sometimes, that is a very hard pill to swallow, but know that he is right there beside you. Like I've mentioned in my first book, *My Heart Shaped Womb,* God chose us to hold this honor to be the parent of an angel. It's a special honor, but a very hard one. Love and hugs, my dear friends.

6

Take a look at yourself in the mirror. If you're like me, I see the face of a woman with PTSD, chronic anxiety and depression disorder. I am NOT ashamed of who I've become, after traumatic events growing up, and then having to bury my only child. These disorders are nothing to be hidden away from society. It's what has made me a much stronger person than I was yesterday. Never be afraid to let someone know when you are hurting. Life is unfair and difficult. No matter the situation, please don't let your smile hide your pain forever. God gives us obstacles in our lives, and the way we handle them is our living testimony that God has our hand in his. We are the light to help those who follow in our footprints. Love and hugs, my friends.

7

Picture a tiny, perfect baby sleeping in the fetal position inside its mother's womb. Now envision a tiny delicate pair of angel's wings. The perfect angel, sleeping so soundly, so peaceful.

Some mornings, it is almost unbearable to get out of bed. Just knowing you have to go through another day, without the one person you wanted the most, who is never going to burst open your bedroom door and jump on top of you asking, "Mommy, what's for breakfast," or, "Can we play outside today?" It's an emptiness that cannot be filled with anything. Sometimes, not even a comforting hug can ease the ache and emptiness left from the child you prayed for, for so long. Just know that God is with you always, and one day, we will be reunited with our sweet babies and it won't matter why they couldn't stay with us. I hope everyone has a blessed day - and remember, you always have a friend in me. Love and hugs.

8

There is a beautiful sculpture in Slovakia dedicated to all unborn children. It's a mother on her knees with her head buried in her hands, obviously sobbing. In front of her is a child - about a toddler's age - with her hand stretched out, gently touching her mother's head. The realism of this sculpture - the mother is in solid white marble, while the little girl is clear glass.

Hello, my friends. I came across this picture while scanning through pictures of angel monuments. I think that it does more than capture the way we felt when we had to bury our child. It actually is a great visual to those who don't really know what child loss looks like. I find it sadly accurate, but comforting. If only we could feel that tiny little hand upon our head. A child never forgotten. A child forever loved. Remember to always speak their name to honor their memory. This sculpture captures our pain in every aspect. Love and hugs, my sweet friends.

9

I chose a beautiful bouquet of soft pinks, baby blues and light peach colors to thank everyone for being a part of *Mothers of Angels,* and in memory of our babies.

A beautiful bouquet to remember our angels. Most people don't like getting flowers because they fade and die, but the way I see it, we are only on this earth for a short time. Since God needed our babies with Him, He left us with beautiful things like flowers and sunsets to remind us he mourns when we mourn. God knows we suffer and grieve. He's our Heavenly Father. So take the time to enjoy the beauty he gives us to remember our precious angels. Love and hugs, my friends

10

Serenity Prayer

God, grant me the serenity to accept the things I cannot change, the courage to change the things I can, and the wisdom to know the difference. Living one day at a time, accepting hardships as the pathway to peace, taking, as HE did, this sinful world as it is, not as I would have it, trusting that He will make all things right if

I surrender to His Will; that I may be reasonably happy in this life and supremely happy with Him forever in the next. AMEN.   - Reinhold Niebuhr

11

I posted a picture of my sweet Shyla.

My friends, I am asking for your prayers today. I've been asking God to place the right words on my heart to describe a very sensitive subject, fur babies. The day after we buried my daughter, the stray tortoiseshell calico - that I had been feeding and making conversations with for five months - jumped in my lap and seemed to know exactly when I needed her. She had never let me touch her until this very moment. So from that point on, I celebrated Shyla's birthday the same day as my daughter's. And involved her in all family functions. She never acted like a cat but presented herself as a stand in for my baby. There were some people who looked at my close bond with Shyla as unnatural or not healthy. Some were more concerned about my sanity if something happened to her. Well, after nearly fourteen years together, God gave her much-deserved angel wings. It was indeed a very traumatic experience - and yes, it was like burying another child. She represented a piece of my Makaylee, and I know Shyla knew that. My point to this story is, if you find yourself closely bonded with a fur baby, and it brings you comfort and peace after losing your child, then don't let ANYONE make you feel bad about letting that sweet critter fill that empty void. I know I never did. This mommy loved both her babies and continues to do so. I just know Shyla is giving Makaylee some of the love I gave her for so many years. Love and hugs, my friends.

You are not a failure or a horrible mother because your child died. You never in your wildest dreams thought that this would ever happen to you. It would not have mattered if you followed every prenatal guideline or altered it a little. Nothing could have changed the outcome of God's plan. I know you have found yourself begging and pleading, just like I have, in hopes that this would be a horrible nightmare. That we could just pray day and night until God might show us some mercy. No matter the circumstances, you were already a wonderful mother. You would have done anything and everything humanly possible to save your child's life, and that already makes you the best mother. And just like me, you would do it all over again just to be that lucky woman chosen to be an angel's mother.

There are still days I feel like a failure, because I couldn't save my baby. But we are not failures. Not by a long shot. We just love so deeply that when something happens that's out of our control, it hurts us even more. I hope everyone has a very blessed day. Love and hugs from *Mothers of Angels*.

12

The very moment our child dies, we are immediately a different person. Someone we are forced to become, not the person we wanted to be but a whole new identity, one not welcomed. I will never be the same person you remember from yesterday. I have the same name, same features, but the old me has wasted away. The pain of losing my child has forever changed me and not for the best. That part of me died with her and was laid to rest. Please don't pity me - I just love my baby like no other. I've become someone so different. I'm a grieving mother.

Hello, my dear friends. Even though this poem rings true for all of us, never forget that you are still a mother. A very special kind of mother, you've been given the toughest parenting position. Remember that Jesus's mother, Mary, had to go through this same journey only to witness her son crucified. But just like Mary, we to can get through this with our faith - and the knowledge that we will be with our little ones when we leave this world. Remember, you're not alone in this. We have one another. Love and hugs to each of you.

13

To my Makaylee and Shyla,

I had a dream last night of you, walking in a field of lilies. Your tiny hand touched all the blooms; your hair was long and wispy.

Stopping briefly at the field's edge, you picked a bloom so pure and white. Smelling the fragrance, God looked at you and said:

"Why the sad face with such beauty in sight"?

You smiled then said; "My mommy loves tulips; but I've looked all around and haven't seen a little bit."

With a twinkle in his eye and a wave of his hand, the lily you were holding became a tulip instead.

You smiled so big and thanked him so; the field turned to tulips, all different colors - bright, beautiful and bold.

As you walked back through the field, a memory must have appeared; for when you stopped with Shyla there, she wiped away the tear. You stroked her fur, and she looked at you with love and so much care.

God knelt down, kissed you both and held you both so near; "Don't be sad my little ones, you'll see your mommy soon. Then you both can walk with her, side by side, amongst the tulips in bloom."

14

Europe has some of the most beautiful and moving statues and monuments to remember their loved ones. I was looking at pictures of some of these stunning works of art and came across one that brought tears to my eyes.

It has to be a family mausoleum, because it is all connected beautifully by an angel, carved out of polished white marble. She is, to scale, the average height of a woman, dressed in flowing robes and long hair. Her wings are very detailed, with each feather etched perfectly. They almost look soft to the touch.

They are gracefully folded down her back, and in her left, arm she's holding a little girl around the age of three or four years. As the angel places her right hand to the entrance of the tomb, the little girl is sweetly nestled against her chest, and her tiny forehead gently rests on her angel's cheek.

Good morning, my friends. I love finding sculptures that capture precious images. I sometimes find them helpful in my grieving process. The one I described above has been one of my favorite ones. I wish I could have something like this at my daughter's resting place.

It speaks volumes, almost comforting to know that there are angels among us, and even when we leave this earth, being led to our Lord and Savior by angels such as this one, it is very soothing.

I printed the picture of this sculpture and placed it in my daughter's memory box because I truly believe, even though she never took a breath on this earth, that her guardian angel lovingly picked her up and carried her home. Love and hugs, my friends.

15

True friendship starts the very second that one person looks at the other and says: "What! You too? I thought I was the only one."

I hope your day is filled with warm memories and the knowledge that you are not alone. You have friends that are on the same road of heartache you are. The road of *Mothers of Angels*. Love and hugs.

16

You know when you have one of those days when you just look up, close your eyes, smile and softly say, "I know that was you."

Have you ever found yourself walking down the street or sitting on your front porch, and a small, light breeze washes over you? It seems to blanket you ever so lightly, almost as if you were floating on a cloud. It feels cool, but still has a warm feeling of a soft hug.

In that brief moment, you feel as if someone is lightly touching your face - leaving love's sweet embrace lingering on your skin. That soft breeze is your angel, giving love's embrace, ever so softly. You breathe it in, letting it consume your body 'til finally, your heart and soul are at peace - leaving a smile on your face, if only for a moment. Love and hugs from *Mothers of Angels*.

17

Dearest Heavenly Father,

I have no words to fully describe my sorrow over the life you chose to take.

I know you're in control over everything, even my heartbreak.

I know my sweet baby is safely nestled in your loving arms,

But I can't help but wish they were in ours.

My mind tells me that we are not truly far apart,

But I wish there was a way you could tell my heart.

I know you grieve when I am sad

And understand that I feel mad.

This loss has been a devastating blow,

To which no one will ever truly know.

I had such dreams for my child you see;

Now I know they will never be.

Please wrap me in your loving embrace

And remind my heart of your amazing grace.

To see me through this horrible tragedy

And let my baby's life lives on through my memory.

I pray all these things in your Holy Name. Amen.

18

I came across a very moving picture of Jesus, gently holding a baby in his arms. The expression on their faces is both comforting and reassuring. It's the look any parent would lovingly give their child.

My dear friends, this picture automatically put my heart at peace. What a wonderful way to be welcomed to our Heavenly home than in our Father's arms. When I was fighting for my life - when my uterus ruptured and the medical team of doctors and nurses were frantically trying to save my life - I had an out-of-body experience. The very last thing I remember is telling someone that I could no longer breathe, and my eyes shut, giving way to the darkness of the unknown. I couldn't tell you how long after I was placed on life support - and transported to emergency exploratory surgery - that I had my little life changing experience, but I remember it like it happened yesterday. It felt like I was being lifted very slowly upwards, and then my eyes opened. All around me was the most brilliant, but soft, white light I have ever seen, accompanied by the feeling of absolute peace. The kind God talks about in the Bible. A peace that passes all understanding, and it truly was, because I looked down and saw my earthly body laid on an operating table, hooked up to multiple machines, and doctors and medical staff from every department, frantically working to save my life. I could not hear a single word being said, or feel anything that was being done to my body, but I can honestly tell you I was surrounded by pure peace.

I felt no sadness, remorse or pain. Just peace, and it was in that moment that I realized I was in the presence of My Lord and Savior. No, I did not get to see his wonderful face, but I knew he was there with me. I don't know how long I was in his presence, but in the blink of an eye, I felt the valiant push of air from the ventilator inflate my lungs, and I knew that I was back in my earthly body.

After my experience, all I could imagine, from that day forward, was how special it was for my daughter to open her eyes for the first time and see her creator. And even though we wish that our faces were the first thing our babies saw, nothing can beat being greeted by Jesus himself. Not having to endure this world, as we have, and see the things we've seen. In more ways than one, I consider that to be the best way to begin a life, even though I still wish I could have met my daughter. Love and hugs, dear friends.

19

Sometimes when the pain of our loss seems too much, I remind myself that my unborn child only knew one thing of this life. It was the faithful and unconditional love I had for her from the second I found out I was to be her mom.

Love, especially unconditional love, seems to be fading as the years go by. The way children are raised this in day and time is proof of that. But for those of us who have lost a child, we know nothing but unconditional love. The type of love we have is never ending and continually grows deeper with every passing moment. We would have gladly begged for our little angels to stay with us where, even outside of our warm and protective womb, our love would envelope them 'til the end of time. Every time that searing ache flows through our hearts when we think of them, that's our unconditional love. A love that no other person could ever recognize, unless they had to say goodbye to something as precious as a child whose life never truly began. Love and hugs.

20

The most humbling picture I've ever seen of mother and child is that of Mary holding Jesus.

Sometimes, we feel like we are the only ones going through the loss of a child. No one else could possibly know the heartache and emptiness we feel when our arms aren't filled with the baby we were so eagerly awaiting. But there is one mother that knew this heartache all too well: Mary. She was given the greatest honor in the whole entire world, as being the mother to the savior of the world.

She was blessed to have seen him grow into the profit God told her he would be. I'm sure she heard about his teachings and healing miracles that changed so many lost souls. How proud she must have been, but also, how scared she must have felt, knowing that one day, her precious son would die for our sins.

Mary endured the hardest loss every imaginable. She witnessed as her son was betrayed, arrested, persecuted, beat by the very people he was going to die for. Then she had to watch helplessly as her son was crucified, alongside two thieves, only to have to bury her beloved son.

I know Mary knew that Jesus would rise from the dead three days later, but still, that had to be the worst experience of her life. The security I get, from seeing a beautiful painting of Mary and baby Jesus, is that we are definitely not the first to endure the death of a child, and we will not be the last. God knows us before we are ever born. He knows every trial and tribulation we will face in our lifetime, and he knows how we will deal with the pains of this world.

He knows our hearts - what they can and cannot handle, and just how capable we are to endure through it, even the death of our own child. God placed many people in Mary's life to help her cope and help keep her faith strong, in that her son's death was never going to be in vain.

We have our faith and promise, from God's word, that we will survive our tragedy, and he also led us to each other here, at *Mothers of Angels,* for the love and support from other parents in mourning. Love and hugs, my dear sweet friends.

21

Lord, I humbly pray

That this page will reach someone today.

To a mother or father in desperate need,

To feel comfort and support from the testimonies they read.

Not only will they know you're there,

But *Mothers of Angels* also cares.

Let them know they are not alone,

That here everyone feels right at home

To unburden their hearts so full of sorrow

To find some hope for a better tomorrow.

Just let them know we've lost children, too,

And we meet here to help each other through.

So, Lord, I once again humbly pray

That this page will reach someone today.

Love and hugs.

22

For each and every grieving parent I meet, I just know that my Makaylee has met their child, and they are playing in heaven - just waiting for us to join them. So, in a way, we are all connected by a special bond, in that we are parents to angels.

Hello my dear friends. I often daydream about my Makaylee and what she may be doing, or who she may be bugging, in heaven. If she's anything like her mother, she has the gift of gab, and by the time I get to heaven, everyone will once again be able to hear the birds sing again. I see her skipping and laughing in wide open fields of wild flowers, all different shades of color. I have no doubt that Jesus is near, keeping watch and joining in the fun from time to time.

When I saw a similar quote as the one above, I envisioned a different daydream, and it was even more breathtaking than the first. As parents who share this difficult task of living with only memories of our babies, I have no doubt that our children have become nothing short of the best of friends.

Playing hide and seek, loving on animals that we can only dream of touching, and coming together to hear Jesus tell them stories of their earthly parents, and how much we love and miss them. But I also know he reassures them that one day, we will all be reunited and have the grandest family reunion ever known to mankind. I pray that everyone has a wonderful day. God bless you all, love and hugs.

23

The truth is that grief never ends; it's forever changing. It becomes a passage in which we take, but not meant for us to stay in forever. Our grief is never a sign of weakness or any fault in our faith. It is, however, the price of unconditional love, and that, my friends, will never end.

Hello, my dear friends. This statement rings true for any type of grief, but the death of a child is, in itself, a whole different category of mourning. I've known grief all my life, with the sudden and very much unexpected death of my mother at a very young age, followed by an abusive first step mother, who used me as a punching bag. But the death of my daughter has been the hardest, most gut-wrenching pain that I've never been able to move past.

Throughout the years, I've often encountered people who have told me not to stay in my grief too long, or if I would just pray a little harder, and whole-heartedly give all my pain and sorrow over into God's hands, that my grief would pass. Well, I can honestly tell you that my Christian walk with God may not be the solid rock it needs to be, but it's definitely not built in the sand. The fact that I conceived my daughter in the first place - after many years of being told I would never be able to become pregnant - was a true miracle in itself. And I know God had his hand in that miraculous blessing, even before I knew I was expecting.

But just like all things in life, nothing is ever free or guaranteed. Just like our Lord and Savior Jesus Christ paid the ultimate sacrifice so that we may be saved by his never-ending grace and spend all eternity in paradise with him. So, too, must we sometimes surrender our happiness for an unknown cause. That is what unconditional love means. It will never get easier or have the happy ending we so desperately prayed for, but sometimes that's the price for love.

Love and hugs from *Mothers of Angels.*

24

Losing a child is not an event; it is a very indescribable wandering of survival.

Today, my husband and I were driving down the streets of our town and went by one of the many churches we have. It's centered in the middle of the older sections of our community. As we were slowly driving by, I noticed a way too familiar site of a funeral service taking place. And like a bolt of lightning, it hit me. I remembered that this was the day a local family was laying to rest their eight-year old daughter, and the services were being held at this particular church. I placed my hand on my husband's leg and told him about the newspaper article I had read, a couple of days before, with this family's tragic story.

As the tears swelled up in the corners of my eyes, I said a silent prayer for the little girl's family and friends that had to endure such a tragic loss. I prayed that God would point them in the right paths to seek help, because surviving this type of loss is crucially important. Never be afraid to seek out counseling, or sometimes medication, to help you make it through this type of loss. It is an unbearable tragedy and something you just don't quickly get over.

Time can sometimes feel like a weight dragging you deeper into its darkness, and sometimes, time itself will seem to stop all together. We feel, as parents, that our lives should end before our children's, so when we lose a child, it disrupts our natural order of things. *Age before innocence,* if I had to put it into words. Life is short and for some, shorter than others, so never take life for granted. Love and hugs, my friends.

25

You ask me if I still cry, well I do.

I wept when you passed away,

I still cry about that every day.

It didn't matter how much, I loved you so;

I couldn't make you stay;

Your heart too pure for us down below.

I watched as they laid you to rest in your tiny grave;

God broke my heart to prove that even true love must go away.

Everyone cries, but there are those of us that tend to cry even more. For us, time heals no wounds, because our hearts have been permanently broken. We sometimes wish that we could hold them one last time, or for those of us who never had the chance to hold our little ones, just to be given that opportunity - would have meant the world. That brief moment that we could have said our goodbyes. We had nothing but tears to compensate for the emptiness we felt in our arms.

Even though God hand-picked our baby to stay in His care,

we were left with broken hearts we've learned to share.

Loving from a distance until we meet again.

So weep when you need to; it shows your love.

May you find some comfort in releasing them.

Love and hugs, my friends.

26

There really are no set guides to surviving grief. You kind of learn as you go. I cannot express enough the importance of showing your grief and frustration after the loss of a child. I know, I tried for years. It cannot be done. Bottling your feelings only compounds the stress and anger you already have. It will always come back and hit you harder. Even though I go to counseling and take medication for depression and anxiety, sometimes I just need to have a good ol' fashioned break down. I've been on the floor, weeping uncontrollably and screaming out, "Why did this happen to me?" or "Why God, why my baby?" Then after I let it all out, I feel just a little bit better, if only for a little while. Don't bottle your heartache, my friend. God will hear your plea, and he will help share your grief. As God said in Matthew 5:4; "Blessed are those who mourn for they shall be comforted." And never forget that *Mothers of Angels* is here for you, as well. Love and hugs.

27

Picture Jesus dressed in white, holding a child gently in a loving hug. *"I can do all things through Christ Jesus who strengthens me."* Philippians 4:13

Good morning, my beautiful friends. I hope this new day finds you at peace. Nothing rings more true than this Bible verse. A lot of people would ask you how your faith can be so strong in Christ when he took your child. Well, I'll tell you even though we would prefer our little ones here with us, God knew that our faith in him would grow stronger through our journey of understanding. People tend to get lost and caught up in everyday life. They become less reliant on God's saving grace to see us through our darkest hours. Learning to lean on Him, and not on our own - understanding builds our trust that He knew what was best for our child way before we did, and that there is a reason for everything God puts us through in our lifetime.

I can honestly say that my faith has grown stronger through my survival process. Without God, nothing is possible, and when you lose a child, He is your number one supporter. Love and hugs, my friends.

28

Everyone is so afraid of dying, until they lose a child. Then, and only then, do we become more afraid of living.

I know that all of us have had this feeling more than once in our lifetime. And I am here to say that this statement, as negative as it may sound to some people, is a very unfortunate reality for a lot of us. Losing a child, suffering from PTSD and chronic anxiety depression disorder are a constant struggle for parents. It's trying to stay optimistic in a pessimistic situation. We truly no longer fear death. In reality, we look forward to seeing our loved ones again, especially our baby.

The death of a child changes everything, altering us both mentally and physically. But know that I am here for you. I know all too well the thoughts and feelings you constantly go through, while others sit by and wonder why you just can't move forward. No, I'm not free from this thought by any means. I still struggle daily, and will continue to do so, 'til I leave this world. But until that time comes, we have one another to lean on, and always have someone to lean on, for support through this heartache called life. Many love and hugs.

29

When I was in nursing school, we learned the stages of the grieving process, and the signs and symptoms to look for in our patients. I wanted to share these with you, because they very much relate to our situation.

1. The overwhelming feeling of tiredness and exhaustion
2. Experiencing confusion
3. Having trouble concentrating
4. Changes in sleep patterns
5. Changes in eating habits
6. Having nightmares
7. Experiencing uncontrollable crying
8. Becoming socially isolated
9. Restlessness
10. Having aches and pains
11. Experiencing bouts of uncontrollable anxiety
12. Finding it hard to breathe

A lot of times, people don't recognize the signs of depression and anxiety. More than likely, it's the person who is going through a traumatic experience. When I lost Makaylee, I was bound and determined that I was not going to let myself sink into depression. But without realizing it, I fell into that dark place and remained stuck there for months. It took my family, taking notice of the dangerous place I was in, for me to get help. Trust me, the traumatic way in which I my baby died still has a profound effect on me, because I almost lost my life, as well.

Things were destined never to be the same for me. Even though I take medication and attend counseling biweekly, I still have that darkness that looms around the corner. But I know that God blessed me with the knowledge that I needed to get help and try to help others. This list of symptoms is nothing to take lightly, so please take heed and get help. That's not weakness. It's your inner strength- and God - letting you know that you can survive this. Love and hugs, my friends. God bless.

30

Hello, my friends. Sometimes we just need to stop and take time to heal. Having anxiety and depression can be very exhausting. When, for no particular reason, your body goes on the defense against itself. Heart pounding, shortness of breath, feeling like you are being suffocated. It's a horrible way to live, and for many of us, it's a sad and all too familiar reality. So just remember to breathe. Take any medications prescribed. Try breathing in some essential oils like lavender, eucalyptus or peppermint. They can be very soothing in a warm bath. Of course, the power of prayer also helps. You are not alone, my friend. Love and hugs.

31

Envision a very steep hillside, and on one side, you see yourself climbing this hill backwards because you are tugging on something very heavy. You look down and see that the rope in your hands is wrapped around a gigantic stone heart, five times your size, possibly weighing several tons. And there is an inscription on the rock which reads: *grief.* The tag attached to the rope is addressed to those around us, and it reads: *Dear family and friends, this is my grief. You can either add more weight to my loss by judging, criticizing and forgetting that I've lost my child, or you can help lighten the load by listening, lending your support and just remembering our loss with us. Which will you choose?*

My friends, for so many of us, this is our reality. We often find ourselves without a positive support system that is needed to help us carry our heartache. Others are so quick to judge and place even more grief on the boulder we are struggling to carry around. If someone in your life is adding to your heavy load, don't be afraid to let them know that you don't need their criticism. You need their love, support and maybe even a little help propping the boulder you carry every day, if only for a little while. That's why I created this group. Even though I have my own boulder of grief to carry around, I also have room in my heart to help others hold their heavy load, if only for a little while. Love and hugs.

32

Trust in the Lord with all your heart and lean not on your own understanding. Proverbs 3:5

Sometimes, even if our faith in God is firmly grounded, we still find it hard to place all our trust in His hands. When tragedy happens, we tend to want control in how we manage through it. Too often, we let our emotions flow freely, and sometimes in desperate situations, that can be dangerous. I know sometimes I wish God would come down from Heaven and just sit, talk and explain to me why he had to take my daughter. Why my mother died when I was only five years old, but I know he can't. That's why he says trust in Him.

Our faith is believing without seeing, but we do see Him. In the hearts and actions of other Christians, and in His word, in which He promises that we will know all the answers when we are called home. I hope everyone has a blessed day. Love and hugs.

33

Our tears are just prayers. They travel from our heart straight to God whenever we can't speak. Psalm 56:8

Today, while checking in on my regular Facebook page, I came across two families that have lost a child today. For those of us that have been on this journey for a while know all too well that for these families, grief has just begun. Sometimes our tears are all we have, and I know that the angels are receiving each tear and feeling how much we love and miss our baby.

So when we need to cry in order to send love to the child we lost just cry. It's good healing for the heart and soul. Plus, our tears are kind of like a special gift from you to your child. And that in itself is priceless. Love and hugs, my friends.

34

From the very moment you left me,

My heart split completely in two.

One side was instantly filled with memories

While the other side died along with you.

I find myself lying awake some nights,

While the world sleeps soundly around me,

And take a stroll down memory lane.

Remembering you is so easy.

I do it every second of every day,

But missing you is the hardest part of heartache

That will never go away.

I hold you tenderly inside my heart

And there you will forever stay.

You see life unfortunately must go on without you

But it will never be the same.

I believe we can all relate to this in one way or another. I've always said that the best part of me died with my Makaylee, and all that is left behind is the shell of the woman I used to be. I know my demeanor has changed. Losing a piece of you will do that. When we are young and our lives begin to thrive, we never think about of the possibility that it can all be taken away in a heartbeat. I think that we should talk about child loss more. Young couples - just starting out in life - don't think about mortality the way we do. If true reality was spoken more often, maybe it wouldn't be such a shock when it happens to someone else. The death of my daughter definitely left tears on my cheeks that will never go away, and like the poem says, life does move on. But for the parents of angels, we are forever stuck in a constant loop of survival. Love and hugs.

35

There is absolutely no moving on; we have been trapped by our love and our grief for the child we lost. Sure, we go through the movements like breathing, laughing. We eat, drink and work.

We manage the everyday things that need to be done, but we stay forever in that second, that minute and the hour that we lost our child. So, move on - to an extent, we have. Our bodies and brains have found a way, but our hearts will remain forever trapped by the love and grief we have for our child.

There is absolutely no way of moving past the death of our child. It consumes you. Every aspect of your life has forever been changed. The hurt makes us feel like an eternal prison for which there is no escape. Sure, it may seem to others that we have accepted our new way of life, but that's only for their benefit.

In reality, our lives have been permanently frozen in time. Remember to just breathe when the world seems to close in on you. We are in this position together. We are a strong and loving group of people, forever bonded by the loss of our child. Love and hugs, my friends.

36

If you know someone who has endured the heartbreak of child loss, and you are uncertain whether to mention it for fear of making the parents feel sad - that saying something in remembrance of their beloved child may be a sad reminder that they died, don't be. For starters, they will never forget what they've lost. You recalling a memory may bring tears, but it also lets them know that you remember their child lived, and that, my friend, is a most precious gift to a grieving parent.

In my book, *My Heart Shaped Womb,* I talk strongly about the importance of remembering our children. Not that we could ever forget. I stress my opinion on this area of grief very often.

I did this in hopes that whoever was reading my words would take them to heart and feel more confident in telling their loved ones to please be patient with us. That being judgmental or opinionated on this delicate matter doesn't help us "get on" with our lives. That if they could show more compassion and empathy in our moments of sadness, it would greatly improve our ability to cope. So don't be hesitant to speak up in honor of your child. You've certainly earned that right. Love and hugs.

37

I found a beautiful picture of a stained-glass window with a cross, and lilies surrounding it. The bold purples and blues are the back drop to show-case the wooden cross. The white lilies are blooming gently against the cross as if they were cradling this sacred symbol of our Savior.

This beautiful picture is a symbol of the love, hope and peace that our Lord has given to us. I recall the beautiful church hymn, "It Is Well With My Soul," written by Haratio Spafford in 1871. He and his wife had five children. Three daughters and a son. At the young age of four, their only son died of scarlet fever. So, to make a new beginning after the great Chicago fire of 1871, Spafford wanted to take his wife and daughters to Europe for a vacation and to help a friend in a mission of ministry. Due to work related issues, Spafford sent his family ahead of him, where he would join them later.

The ship that his wife and daughters were on collided with another ship, and all three of Spafford's daughters were lost at sea, along with 223 other souls on board. Mrs. Spafford was found barely alive, along with 47 survivors. She contacted her husband with the devastating news, and he boarded the next ship to get to his wife.

When the ship Spafford was on came to the place where the sinking had taken place, the captain brought Mr. Spafford on deck. He found it hard to sleep that night and said, "It is well, God's will be done." He later wrote the beautiful hymn we now sing in almost every church. With such an inspirational story, that is full of complete sorrow. It is written proof that we to can survive our tragedies, that God is with us always, even in our darkest hours. Love and hugs.

38

I wanted to take a moment to thank each and every one of you for joining me in my quest to help others. I know that you all have given me a reason to get up in the morning. I'm always honored that all of you have shared your stories with me. I know that I'm not alone.

It brings my heart comfort knowing that we can all come together and show support for one another. God has truly blessed me with all of you, and we are forever united in a unique bond that I feel will stay strong 'til we are called home. Our children are all smiling down on us for remembering their lives. No matter how long or how short. Love and hugs, my dear friends. Love and hugs.

39

The hardest loss any one person can possibly suffer - to survive through - is the death of their child.

The whole tragedy not only changes you, it slowly demolishes you, and for the rest of your life, you nurse a wound that will never be healed.

Almost every single day since we said goodbye to our babies, our souls do feel demolished.

The emptiness and hurt we feel leaves us completely drained and forever trapped in a never-ending circle of feeling lost. Sure, as the years go by quickly for others, for us, it merely creeps by. Taking its sweet time, doing its best to keep reminding us that grief is our constant companion.

Some people will never have to endure this kind of lifestyle change, but we have to rearrange our entire way of thinking - just to survive. The emptiness left by our hopes and dreams that we had planned for our babies was forever altered when they had to go.

But have hope, because when we are reunited with them, we can spend eternity living out those unfulfilled dreams to our hearts desire. Love and hugs, dear friends.

40

The Realities of Loss

The loss of a child is as bad as you think. Nothing anybody can do or say can change that fact. Our baby cannot come back again, what's done is gone. There is no beauty in death. We can acknowledge death in everything. We can feel its pain and sadness. But it will never be made right this side of Heaven.

Your grief is experienced differently than those around you. For everyone grieves differently. In life, there are some pains that can never be cured by a smile or kind word. There are no solutions to be found, and you need only to move through your sorrow at your own pace, not that of others. You don't need everyone criticizing or commenting on how they would handle their grief. Just acknowledge our loss.

For those around us that have never had to bury a child, reading this would be a great starting point. The death of a child is like no other. Nothing can prepare you for what you will endure in the coming months.

It is a completely different type of loss. Most people would look at our loss as just another life event. Like a grandparent or someone who has lived a full life has passed, and the pain we feel will lessen with time - but it doesn't, not by a long shot.

If anything, it seems to intensify as time comes and goes. The dark hole left - that we stare into - is filled with what might have been. Lost hopes, lost dreams and a love that will never be felt by a hug. There is no beauty in a child's death, and this is true, for the beauty that was to be is now a part of Heaven. We see it with every sunrise and sunset. Love and hugs.

41

Food for thought, for a parent that feels free to pass their wisdom on child loss, when they've experienced it personally. Think before you speak to a parent in mourning about being grateful for the child or children they still have, or that they can try again. For some parents, having another child will never happen, and those of us that have been blessed with other children, we are very grateful we have them, but here's a question to think about. Which one of your children could you live without? Just some food for thought.

Hello, my dearest friends. Like always, I found myself thinking back to the time after Makaylee died. At the very beginning of my grief, I did have thoughts like the ones I mentioned above.

Consumed by my own selfishness, I would say these exact words to other parents, not really stopping to think that maybe they, too, had experienced child loss. As I have been living with my sorrow for nearly fourteen and a half years, I've heard about and seen families, who have several children, lose one.

Instinctively, my heart hurt for them, but I knew that they had the blessings of their other children to help cope with the loss of one. I hated those dark days in my life. It became even harder to not have thoughts like this whenever I realized that I would never be a mother again. An earthly mother, that is.

But I've grown in my grief, if that makes any sense. I have become more open minded about the way I see things. Sure, the hurt is still there when others say these words to me. That will never change. I miss my Makaylee more and more with each passing day.

I have prayed for forgiveness and know that God understands my thoughts. But if this quote has anything to teach us, it's that no one should ever say hurtful things to a grieving parent. The thoughts and feelings we have during our grief are just our way of defending ourselves against the world. I do, however, think that, for parents who are blessed to have all their children safe and sound, please be aware that there are no certainties in life.

It can change in half of a heartbeat. A grieving parent, no matter if they have other children or not, are always on the defense in making sure that the child they did lose will not be forgotten. God bless all of you, my dear friends. Love and hugs.

42

I found an image of a woman pregnant with her child, and the picture shows the mother from a front-facing position with her arms and hands cradling her abdomen. The artist who drew this picture truly captured the beauty of motherhood by allowing us to see the beautiful baby nestled inside its mother's womb. A pair of tiny angelic wings have been placed on the baby's back, and the caption reads: *Do you believe in angels, because I do. I grew one next to my heart.*

The beauty and heartache of this picture captures more than the raw reality of being a mother to an angel. It captures the very essence of what we have had to endure. The gentle and caressing way the mother so lovingly has her arms cradling her unborn child while they sleep in the safe confines of her womb. I think all babies are angels, gifts sent from God. Some are born with transparent wings while others, like our babies, spread their wings in flight to Heaven when God calls them home. Regardless, we carry them close to our hearts forever, and even though their hearts beat only for a short time, they will continue to beat forever in ours. Letting go of them physically was out of our control, but no one can ever take away the memories we made with them while they lived.

Even if it is through ultrasound pictures, and forever hearing the quick thumping of their little heartbeats, those are for- ever and completely ours to treasure. Even though I miss my Makaylee beyond comprehension, I do feel a little bit of honor, knowing God chose her to be one of his angels. It will never get easy for us. This life we live will always be full of heartache and uncertainty, but we can have some peace knowing that even for a short time, they heard our heartbeat while we heard theirs. And I know they felt the unconditional love we had - and still have - for them, if only for the brief moment in time our hearts were intertwined. Love and hugs, my sweet friends.

43

Heavenly Father,

I can-not find the words to express the amount of sorrow that I feel from this loss. I know that you are in complete control and have my precious baby in your loving arms this very moment. I need for my heart to understand that you are grieving with me. I know you hurt when I hurt, and you rejoice when I rejoice. Please comfort me, dear Lord, show me you care, and help my heart learn to accept the path I've been given. Amen.

44

Anytime a child is lost, we just don't lose them at that moment. We lose so much more than that, we lose every moment we were to have with them. Past, present and future.

When I was pregnant with my daughter, I never had the joy of feeling her move. The doctors were amazed at this, because - with having two uteruses and my daughter being in the smaller of the two, they thought for sure that I would be feeling my apparently very active child moving around. Sometimes, I'm grateful to have been spared that special time during my pregnancy, and other times I feel cheated. At five months along, usually, its precious moments like this that are imprinted on our hearts. After her death, I found myself recalling where every piece of furniture sat in her nursery.

I mourned wholeheartedly, knowing the fact that I would never hear the sound of her first cry of life. Her stumbled first steps or her first word - which I had already figured out it was going to be pizza - because that's all I wanted while I was pregnant. I would never see her first day of school, hearing about what she learned that day. Helping her get ready for her first school dance or her graduations.

These memories were all God's now. There is not a single day that goes by that my heart doesn't ache for another chance to have these experiences. When friends or loved ones question the depths of our grief, gently remind them that all our most treasured memories are locked safely away in our hearts, and that's an ache we relive every day for the rest of our lives, for the first time. Love and hugs, my friends.

45

I beg you, please be patient with me.

I've lost someone so precious, as tiny as can be.

The child I prayed for, and wanted so much,

Has gone to heaven beyond my touch.

And tough times may fly by for you and others;

I relive it every day because I'm their mother.

When we lose a child, we are constantly aware that something is always missing. I know that I'm reminded daily of my Makaylee's death, every time I see the scar on my lower abdomen.

It is a constant reminder of what I don't have in my life. I don't mean to leave the fathers out, but for mothers, we learn to accept the changes our bodies go through during pregnancy. Constantly bonding with the child growing in our womb, always worrying about their development and praying for a safe and healthy delivery, and a healthy baby. Being sick with our constantly changing bodies, and if everything goes smoothly, we worry about the pain and the unknowns of impending labor.

For those of us whose babies never took a breath outside the safe confines of our wombs, we have the horrible experience of miscarriage, or having to carry our angel 'til they are full term.

Either way, it leaves a permanent mark - not just on our bodies, but also on our hearts. We blame ourselves for our child's death, even though we know it was never in our control to begin with. So for us, it is a second-by-second existence.

We never have to be reminded of the reality that our babies will never look at us and smile, or say, "I love you, Mommy."

We have scars for that, both inside and out, both mentally and physically. So indeed, be patient with us. We are struggling with demons much deeper than the loss itself. Love and hugs, my dear friends.

46

Some people will say that you are too painful to remember; I say to them you're too precious to ever forget.

I know each and every one of us have had someone in our lives that. at one time or another. have let negative words slip out in regards to the memory of our child. I can honestly tell you that this has happened to me too many times to count. I would get so angry and defensive. because their words were so hurtful. and it was becoming hard to keep my mouth shut.

I just learned to choke back the tears and come to the realization that my baby's memory remained alive only through me. I really became enraged when they would say that talking or thinking about my daughter was too painful for them.

Well, one day I woke up and decided that other people's feelings towards my daughter's memory was not my problem. and felt it was downright disrespectful for others to voice their opinion on how I mourned her, since I was the one who carried her and almost died having her.

So since that day, I have worked hard in keeping my daughter's memory very much alive and in the present, and not in the past. I made a memory keepsake box that has her footprints, the last sonogram picture of her and a little angel rabbit that a labor and delivery nurse gave to me.

On my bedroom dresser, I have a vase of pink silk roses, along with one of the bears that was on a flower arrangement from her funeral. I also have a picture of her headstone, in a picture collage that has the word *family* carved in the frame.

A lot of people would say that having these things around all the time isn't healthy, but I say that not having these things around is not healthy. Your baby was a part of you and your family. They did exist, and their memory will never be forgotten, even if we are the only persons to speak their name. They will always be important, never forget that. Love and hugs.

47

Imagine being all alone on a beach. The breeze is blowing through your hair, and while you sit on the cool sand, you bring your knees up to your chest and look out at the vast open sea in front of you. Just you and your thoughts.

Sometimes, we find ourselves feeling like the person I described above. Sitting all alone and starring out into a vast sea of uncertainty - figuratively speaking. Some days, after we wake up and start our day, we find ourselves caught in a never-ending sea of sadness. The pieces left behind, after our baby leaves this earth, seem to no longer fit together.

It doesn't matter how hard we force ourselves to make the scattered pieces come together - to resemble some of our life before our tragedy - there's just no way a square peg will fit in a round hole. And a puzzle will never be whole again without all the pieces. All we can do is learn to place the broken pieces of our hearts into God's hands and let him mold them together with the memories we hold so dearly.

Just like looking out at the horizon that touches the endless sea of our grief. One day we will have the missing pieces of our heart returned to us. We can once again put them together and enjoy the sea that touches the horizon, except there will be no uncertainty, only eternity with our children.

Until that day, always remember you have a friend in me, and even though I have broken and lost pieces in my heart, together we can help each other in keeping the pieces we do have as close as possible. Love and hugs, my friends.

48

Even though a child dies, the parent still has a connection to that child. It matters not the age they were called home or how long ago they left; they are forever bonded soul to soul.

That's the true unconditional love of a parent. It is more powerful than death, and even though the heart breaks with sorrow from the loss, the love a parent carries for that child remains untouched.

Unconditional love - what a wonderful thing to have. What an honor to have the opportunity to experience it. That's what we have with our angels from the moment we find out we are pregnant. It's a love that grows more with every second that we carry them.

We are truly bonded for all eternity, and nothing, not even their death, will sever this connection. Even though we know God has them safely in His keeping, we still worry. When I go to the cemetery, I feel connected to my daughter. I take my time in washing her headstone and all her figurines that have been given to her through the years.

I always place a new flower arrangement and talk to her - about everything that has been going on in my life, and how much I miss her. But I always get sad when it's time to say goodbye, because I feel like I'm leaving her behind, and it kills me every time.

It's almost beyond unbearable, and sometimes it takes all the strength I have to not just stay with her. That's unconditional love.

The silver lining of this, which is so hard for us to understand, is that our angels feel how much we love them, and nothing, not even the separation of death, can ever alter that. Love and hugs, my friends.

49

Have you ever closed your eyes and wished that you could wake up, and this is all a very bad dream? Me, too.

This is the everyday reality that we live in as parents of angels. When I woke up, a day and a half after losing my daughter, on life support in the ICU, I didn't need anyone to tell me that my Makaylee was gone. I already knew. But that never stopped me from wanting it all to be a bad dream. I would relive my nightmare every time I would close my eyes. For many months following my traumatic loss, I refused to close my eyes. Reality was not an option.

Of course, as the days turned into weeks, then months and finally years, I came to the realization that it didn't matter if I closed my eyes or not, my daughter was not coming back.

I know we all wish that we could wake up from this nightmare we are living, but as we know all too well, it will never happen. All we can do is believe in our faith and do the best we can to survive this unwanted lifestyle, until God calls us home.

I know it's not easy, my friends, but just put one foot in front of the other and take a deep breath, and know that you're not going through this alone.

So close your eyes and rest, for tomorrow is only a day away. We can't change what happened to us, but we can live our lives in the security of God's promise that we will see them again. Much love and hugs, my friends.

50

Sadly, we will never truly heal, and the pain will never lessen with time. But in time, we learn to embrace our loss within our hearts and realize that the world will never fully understand our heartache. Life, we come to realize, is selfish and expects us to heal completely, but that will never happen. We will manage the best way we know how and live through our grief, one day at a time.

By now, you all have seen the how I like to write poems and have you envision beautiful pictures that represent how I feel. That's a big reason I started *Mothers of Angels*.

I speak openly about the loss of my only child and try to inspire others to navigate through their grief. Not to get over it, but to live with it the best we can. Our grieving process is never going to get easier with time. It does, however, become tolerable to some extent. Society wants us to pick up where we left off as if our loss never happened.

Family and friends seem to keep silent on the memory of our babies, and we are told to accept the cards we've been handed. Well, truth be told, we've been given the crappiest hand of cards to play in this game of life. If society would open their eyes and hearts - just a little bit - when it comes to understanding our grief, then life might seem a little less heartless.

I've always said we live through the pain and loss of our babies second by second, not day by day. It forever changes. Some days will be tolerable, while others will completely be devastating. A never-ending cycle of uncertainty. Just know that you never have to go through this alone. *Mothers of Angels* was created to help parents, like me, know that there is still plenty of human compassion left in those of us who are forever bonded in our grief. Love and hugs.

51

A mother naturally protects her child. But a grieving mother has to fight to protect her child's memory.

I know everyone in this group has fought this battle many times. Keeping our child's memory alive or protecting it.

Sometimes, it can feel like a never-ending battle. For people who have never had to bury a child, it is virtually impossible for them to fully understand the importance of keeping an angel baby's memory alive.

A lot of people feel that once someone is buried, they are gone, so they rarely say their name or speak of the life they had.

And I know people mourn differently, but to those of us that have had to sit under that funeral canopy, just staring at the tiny casket that has your whole world closed inside, we need to have something to cling to.

Even if our babies never drew breath outside the womb, we still want everyone to know they were here, if only for a little while.

So please don't let anyone tell you that talking about your loss, or the little time you did have with your child, isn't healthy. Our babies mattered; they still do and always will.

Memories are all we have, and personally, I've come to realize that speaking about our angel is a very important part of our healing. And if people think otherwise, then the door is always open so they can leave. Protect your baby's memory. Love and hugs.

52

After you have a child who is in heaven, you live in a world between here and there.

This is definitely the way we find ourselves living. We are stuck in a never-ending limbo between this earth and wanting to be with our babies. The pull from both sides sometimes is equal, but most of the time, our grief sways us in wanting to be with the child we lost. And it's not that we don't care about our loved ones here on earth, but sometimes, our broken hearts yearn to be with our child. It's a never-ending roller coaster ride that keeps us in a constant loop of heartache.

Some days are tolerable, while others, we find ourselves falling completely and utterly apart. While living here, we are constantly reminded of our loss, and the pain increases daily while we find ourselves thinking about being reunited with our little one.

Finally getting to hold them and feel the joy their hug brings. Living in this dark limbo is a hard burden to bear; it's cruel and unforgiving. It feels like a punishment and a life sentence for which we can never get overturned. Stay strong, my friends. Balance these two hurtful worlds the best way you know how. It will never be easy, and some days it will feel down right unbearable, but together we can stay strong. Love and hugs, my sweet friends.

53

My little one, you are my very first thought when I rise in the morning, and you are my final thought as I go to sleep, because you are my never ending, beautiful, most precious story.

Every story has a beginning and an ending. It's the words spoken, or unspoken, that define us. In life, everyone starts out with a blank sheet of paper. What we do and accomplish along the way shows our unique personalities. But when life throws obstacles in our path like the death of our child, our stories change drastically. It's almost like the pages before our loss disappear and seem meaningless. Starting over with our life's story is very hard to do. Sometimes, you just want to erase the newest pages and pray that, tomorrow, you can wake up and start all over again. While parents who have children get to add memories to their pages, we are left with blank pages.

We are constantly reminded that a big part of them is in Heaven. Our minds constantly rely on every detail of our child's story, and it does stick with us day and night. A never-ending cycle of heartbreak, and not a second goes by that we don't think about our little ones.

Morning, noon and night are occupied by thoughts of our sorrow and guilt. But starting our new chapters can be a great way to helping us with recovery.

So it's okay to have our babies in our thoughts every second of every day. Before going to sleep at night and waking up the next day, just remember your story is not finished. God has a plan, and he will guide your pen in continuing your story. Love and hugs.

54

All my life I had the notion that grief was a sad time that followed a traumatic life event or death, and in order to move past the tragedy, you had to push through. But I'm learning that grief is something you simply cannot push through, but have to absorb the acceptance. Grief is not just something you complete or find the ending to. It is not a task that you must finish by a certain time and just move on from. It transforms you from the inside out, altering everything in your life, forcing you to see life in a new light.

My friends, there is no other side to grief. Especially after you prayed and yearned for the baby you once carried. After many years of wanting to be a mother, to experience the joys of parenthood, even the hard times that we see our family and friends have with their children. The dreams you had of everything that is never to be. That is the reality we are left with - a bottomless hole in our hearts that cannot be mended. We are forever changed from what could have been. Your heart breaking every time you see a child of any age, wondering what your baby would look like, or what they would be doing.

Looking at family photos, and seeing the vacant spot where your child would be, hurts tremendously. Knowing that your loss has become a constant companion that pulls at the very essence of your being. Reminding you that you will never have those precious moments to turn into memories, as others in your life have been able to do. So no, there is no other side of grief after child loss. It's only learning to navigate through everyday life the best way we know how. And learning how to breathe again, even though you feel smothered by your immense pain, can be very hard to do. All we can do is be there for one another, sharing the oxygen of just surviving. Love and hugs, my friends.

55

The hardest and unfair game called grief can leave you feeling the weakest you have ever felt before, forcing you to morph into the strongest person you will ever become.

Grief is indeed a very nasty game of having multiple emotions hit you all at once, leaving you feeling extremely exhausted - both mentally and physically. It consumes every aspect of your daily life and doesn't care if you are having a good or bad day. Having memories of the baby - that will never be - constantly replays over and over again in your head, while your heart tries to understand all the overwhelming pain that never ends.

You slowly become someone you no longer recognize when you look in the mirror. Where a happy expectant mother used to gaze upon her changing body in anticipation is now a hollow shell of a woman, left with nothing but endless grief for what might have been. With time, you find yourself becoming someone you never wanted to be. But in a small way, the pain we carry makes us stronger - whether we realize it or not. Even though we break down every day and think ourselves weak, I believe we are the strongest people I know. We've managed to find a way to keep living after the death of our child, and that is not an easy way to live. Stay strong, my beautiful friends. Together, we can conquer this weakness that plagues us relentlessly. Love and hugs.

56

Not one single person has the right to condemn you on how you put back the broken pieces of your heart, or how long you should take to grieve. For no one knows how deep your pain goes, and recovering the tiny pieces will take time - and an abundance of it. Because no one heals the same way, it is a learn as you go.

No one has the right to tell us how long to mourn or how to go about doing it. Everyone copes differently, just like everyone grieves differently. God made us in his image, but with our own unique personalities. Grief has no time frame, and definitely no limits. For those of us who have lost a child have every right to feel sad for as long as we want without being judged or criticized. We have earned every inch of our healing process, and I think we should be shown the respect to do what we feel necessary to get through this tragedy. What a lot of people fail to remember is that the death of a child is a lifelong sentence. It's like being stuck in a prison of emotional instability, where one minute you are okay, and then in the blink of an eye, your whole world can come crashing down upon you, leaving you stuck in the middle, feeling helpless to escape. So, deal with your grief - the best and only way you know how to.

There is no right or wrong way to mourn, and trust me, there is no time limit on how long you choose to miss your child. So, cry, scream, feel angry at the world and those in it. Whatever helps you feel just a little bit better, stick with it. You've lost a child, and that's a whole other level of pain and grief. Love and hugs, my friends.

57

You know when you hurt - whether you see a loving mother caring for her child the way that you would have with yours, or watching a careless mother neglect her child, knowing that you would never take for granted the precious times with your angel.

Nothing upsets me more than a mother who mistreats her children. As a nurse, I've seen a lot of this, and every time a baby would be admitted for failure to thrive, I would often find them crying out for attention, and they had been for quite some time, because their voice had become hoarse. While the mother was passed out in the bed, their baby would be laying helplessly in their own filth and craving human affection. It broke my heart in two.

Since then, I have really had a major problem with child abuse and neglect. After Makaylee died, I found myself becoming more frustrated with the mistreatment of children. I felt anger towards God for allowing these people to have multiple babies and not care whether they lived or not. Here I was, begging for a second chance at motherhood, because I would never abandon my child. I knew that if God had allowed my Makaylee to live, everything I did would be for her.

I would have moved mountains so she could walk without obstacles. I wouldn't have been a helicopter parent, but I sure wouldn't have taken her life for granted. You can't help but ask *why* sometimes. It seems unfair that our precious baby would have never wanted for anything, especially our love from them. I just have to pray hard and remind myself that I'm not the mother that will have to answer for the miss treatment of one of his precious gifts. I would say I'm sorry for being so outspoken and on my soapbox about this, but to be honest, I'm not. I know that for those of us who have had to stare blankly at a tiny coffin, with our precious gift closed inside, we would give anything to have just one more day with the baby we love so deeply.

Love and hugs, dear friends.

58

Sometimes it's hard to know what hurts more. Seeing a loving and doting mother who nurtures her child, the way you should be with your child, or seeing a careless mother who takes for granted her child by neglecting them?

I can honestly say nothing upsets me more than a mother who mistreats her child. When I practiced as a nurse, I saw my share of babies admitted with a diagnosis of failure to thrive. Being a survivor of child abuse, I have a very low tolerance for any parent who would put their own selfish wants and needs in front of their child's. After my daughter died, well, you can only imagine how short my fuse became when I had precious babies admitted to the hospital, and I would find a very mal-nutritioned, unkempt child that needed nothing more than a warm bath, a bottle, clean clothes and someone to cuddle them.

I often found myself becoming angry with God as to why he took my daughter away from me, when it was obvious that these parents were not worthy of the precious gift God had bestowed upon them. Children are a gift, even when they are called home. If Makaylee would have lived, everything I did would have been for her. If I had to, I would have moved mountains to make sure she wanted for nothing. I would have tried my best not to be a helicopter parent, but I sure wouldn't have taken her life for granted.

You can't help but ask, "why," because it seems so unfair. Because you know your angel would have never wanted for anything, especially your love for them. I just have to bow my head and pray very hard, and remind myself that I'm not the mother that will have to answer for the treatment - or lack thereof - towards his most precious gift. I would say that I'm sorry for being on a soapbox about this, but I would be lying.

I know all of us that have had to stare at our child's casket, with our precious gift closed inside, would give anything to have them snuggled soundly in our arms with nothing but unconditional love, and all the attention we could possibly give them. They would never be taken for granted. Love and hugs, friends.

59

Unless you have lost a child in your lifetime, you will never understand the grief, and the life sentence, that is placed on the parents.

Doesn't this hit you right in the heart? I mean, if outsiders are looking for a visual of a little piece of what we feel like every single day of our lives, then this would be a small start. A lot of people forget that, while they move on with their day, this is what we wake up to every single day. Except, we can't remove the bars that keep us confined; we can't just go in front of a judge and jury to plead for our babies to be given back to us.

There is no relief from our heartache due to good behavior, and we are not given a parole officer to help carry our pain. Our loss keeps us in solitary confinement, with a life sentence that will never be revoked.

We will forever remain walking our personal green mile, 'til the end of time. So, the next time someone asks you what it feels like to live without your baby, just use this quote for your response, and then tell them to multiply that feeling tenfold. God bless you, my friends. Love and hugs.

60

Imagine your favorite flower. Now make a beautiful bouquet displaying the beautiful colors, while the soft aroma fills your senses with a calming fragrance.

Life is forever changing, with every season bringing its own unique colors and smells. I fully believe that our angels are helping our heavenly father create these unbelievably beautiful works of art. I think it is our baby's way of showing their love for us in the most unique way. Even sunrises and sunsets are a reminder that they are with us.

What a precious gift to wake up to. One day, we will be able to share in this experience with them while making up for lost time.

So, take some time during the day and enjoy the beauties of nature. Your child works hard to show you their love.

61

I used to think that I needed to keep my heart's brokenness hidden until my life was somewhat back together. But I couldn't have been more wrong. The people that make the biggest impact in this great big cruel world need to share their brokenness. No matter how shattered, messy or uncomfortable it may make others feel, life is unfair and harsh. It doesn't come in a pretty covered package.

Believe it or not - in our wounds, there is some beauty to its existence. You just have to carefully look. For those of us who have had to become brave after great loss, we know that you cannot live by man's rules of "fake it 'til you make it."

Throughout time, not much has changed when it comes to keeping sealed lips when it comes to child loss. There is no such thing as a perfect time or place to discuss such a delicate subject. Sweet babies are called home, every second of every day, all over the world. When we go through the loss of a child, I fully believe that the loss should be talked about - just as if your baby had lived, and we talked about how precious they were lying in our arms. I think today's younger generation has no clue that having a baby, even in this modern time of medication, can still be very dangerous.

Last year, a young, healthy friend of mine had a pretty normal textbook pregnancy, but despite proper prenatal care and taking good care of herself, she went into labor and, shortly after her baby was born - perfectly healthy, she died suddenly. A silent killer known as a placenta embolism occurred shortly after she gave birth.

It is a rare condition, and most of the time, very quick. It occurs when a piece of the placenta breaks away from the uterus and travels into the mother's blood stream. Usually, by the time symptoms present themselves - low blood pressure, profuse bleeding - it's too late, and unfortunately, my friend died, shortly after giving birth to her child. She was able to see her beautiful baby and cradle him, for a few short minutes, before she succumbed to her failing body.

No one ever wants to talk about the dangers of child birth and how unpredictable it is for both mother and child. But for parents like us, we know - all too well - that nothing is for certain, and no life is guaranteed. We have the chance to change the stigma and help educate others. In honor of our precious angels that have gone on before us. Love and hugs.

62

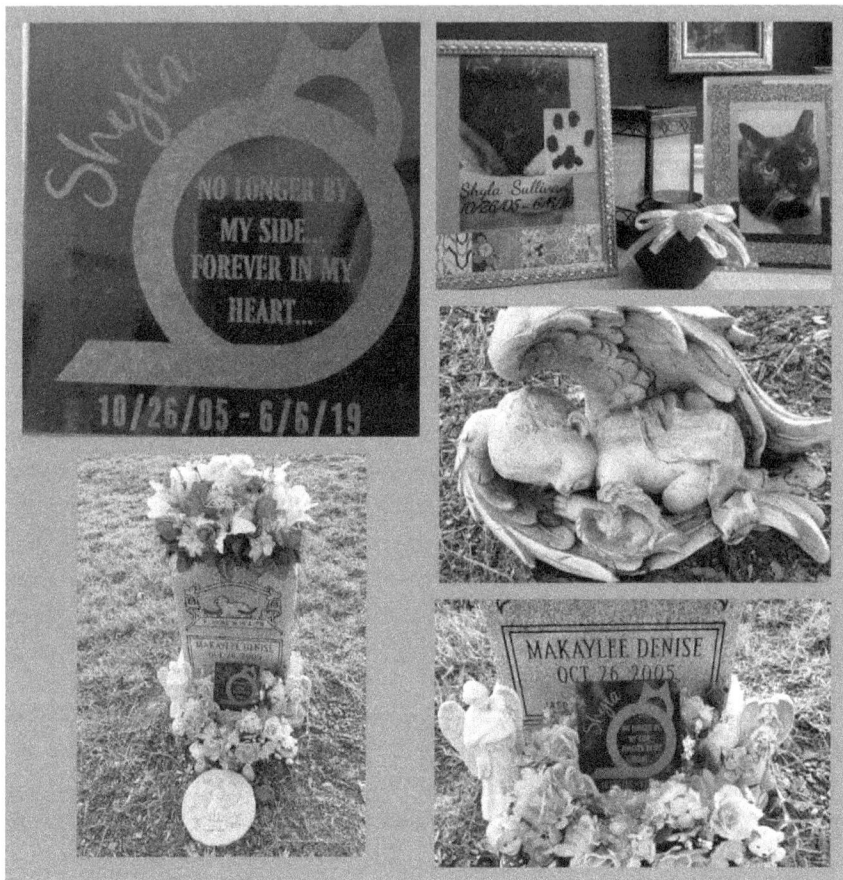

In honor of pregnancy and infant loss awareness month, we remember. We remember all the babies born, sleeping safely in their mother's womb. We honor the babies that we carried close to our hearts, but never in our arms. For the sweet little angels we held in our arms but had to let go, and for the sweet angels that did come home but could not stay.

October is when we hold a special day aside to remember all the little lives that blessed us so much, if only for a short time. It's also the month I lost my beloved Makaylee. As I mentally prepare myself for her upcoming fourteenth birthday, I'm also trying to prepare my heart for honoring my beloved Shyla, my four-legged angel. She came to me as a wild cat and made her forever-presence known the day after Makaylee's funeral. I have no doubt God made her, just for me, at just the right moment.

She never acted like a cat, but presented herself as my baby. This will be her first birthday in heaven with her sister. The thought of my two sweet precious babies, together in heaven, does bring some warmth to my heart, but it also leaves a huge hole that cannot, and will not, be mended.

As the days of this month go by, even through our own grief, let's pray and remember those parents that are just starting their journey. and even though there are no words to be said that will bring our children back, a thought and a prayer goes a long way. my friends. Big love and hugs to you all.

63

Even though our babies are not here physically, they are here always in our hearts, helping us envision a beautiful story that might have been.

My Makaylee is always on my mind. I never stop wondering what she would look like at age fourteen. I know she would be going to school dances and probably having a couple of boys wanting her to be their girlfriend. Missing out on these exciting experiences of trying on dresses, getting her hair curled and pulled up. Watching her make her grand entrance, and watching her daddy tear up with pride at his beautiful daughter. I have no doubt that she would have looked gorgeous in anything she put on. My heart aches for these memories that I have missed out on - that now only exist in my dreams. I will always have these beautiful thoughts to cherish, as should every parent to an angel.

Dreams are meant for everyone, especially when that's all you have left. Treasure every moment you have with the children you do have, and hold on to the ones you have safely tucked away in your heart - of the angel that would have been. Love and hugs.

64

It's perfectly all right to be upset, aggrieved and stranded. It is also acceptable to feel unbalanced, isolated and tormented. Crying is perfectly natural, and not being okay with anything is perfectly all right. Most importantly, go easy on yourself, and stay away from negativity and those who influence it. You are already fighting a never-ending battle within yourself, so don't let others become extra barricades to overcome.

Since our child died, we have had people tell us not to be angry or upset for too long, because it just isn't healthy. What they forget to understand is that we still go through periods of feeling guilty for not being able to protect our babies, so they could stay here with us. With time, we do lose a little bit of that guilt, just because we learn to accept that it was completely out of our hands. But we don't need anyone's opinion on how to feel or how long we should feel it.

Sincerely remind them that it was you, not them, that physically and emotionally carried your baby and then tragically lost them without warning. That it was you that sat in front of the tiny casket, wondering why this was happening to you. Let them know that their opinions may stem from good intensions, from their point of view, but from our stand point, they have reminded us of all the grief that clings to us, every second of every day.

We don't need other people's "opinion," we just need some empathy. We'd prefer for their words to be sincere, but if they can only put on a falsetto form of compassion, then that would be more helpful than being negative. The words and actions of others greatly increase our defenses and anxiety with the internal war we struggle to fight every day.

Having a positive and loving group, such as this one, is good medicine for the grieving soul. Together, we can push out all the negativity from others, and at least, win one small battle of our never-ending war. Much love and hugs, my friends.

65

How is it that you love someone whom you've never met, or never will meet? How do you envision the precious face that you never got to see? How can you mourn the life of someone that never got to live? Well, it's simple; a mother's love for her child takes root way before they start forming in their womb. When we hear their tiny heartbeats for the very first time, that love intensifies ten-fold and continues to do so throughout our pregnancy.

Even if our little one never took a breath on this earth, they still lived. And we love them for as long as we live, just like they have always been here.

No matter how long we have been in mourning for our baby, people find a way to ask the question, "WHY?" It's quite simple really, because we love them - that is why. Notice I said, "love," and not, "loved." Unconditional love never goes away, and while some of us only get to see our babies on a monitor screen during an ultrasound, we instantaneously fall head over heels for the tiny life we are growing.

The love we feel, after we hear that beautiful sound of life inside us, grows more and more with each passing moment. The next time someone asks you how you love and mourn so deeply over someone you never got to meet, tell them that, even though you never had the chance to gaze into the beautiful eyes of your child that you protected inside your womb, no matter how long or short the time, you DID know them.

You were connected from day one, and that bond, along with your love, will never fade with time. In fact, it only seems to get stronger as time goes on. Love and hugs.

66

You are strong, even though you may feel completely broken. The fact that you are able to hold yourself together - and move forward - is amazing in itself. Never stop; never give up. You are forever healing, and no one ever said it had to be a pretty process, or even graceful, for that matter. All that truly matters is that you keep going.

We are strong! Period. End of discussion. We are living through the most difficult heartbreak anyone can suffer. Just breathing is a great accomplishment, and holding our heads up while others show no empathy well that's just down right amazing. Strong in the way we strive to honor our angels' memories. The remarkable way we can weep endlessly, to the most inner core of our souls and still manage to get out of the bed the next morning, is unbelievable in itself.

To yearn, without hope of a miracle, for the child we so much wanted and would have moved Heaven and Earth for. Even walk through fire, if it meant their lives would have been spared. So yes, WE ARE STRONG. More so than most people realize. They think of us as weak or broken, but our shoes would be too large - and too heavy - for them to wear. God chose us because he knew we were fighters, and because we love whole heartedly. Love and hugs, my friends.

67

What does a grieving mother need?

I need to speak my child's name without everyone crying,

For my child's life to be counted with all the other children, grandchildren and great grandchildren,

To feel some empathy on birthdays and anniversaries;

I sometimes need to stay in bed, and sometimes I need encouragement to get out of it.

Sometime just a hug would be nice, without commentary;

I need to be asked if I'm okay and for you to be able to handle the true answer.

MOTHERS OF ANGELS

I need for family and friends to carefully announce pregnancies, baby showers, births because mine didn't happen.

My heart can take a lot, but it is also fragile, so handle with some care.

My emotions have been taken on a never-ending roller coaster ride;

I ask for patience while I mourn, for however long I need to, even if it's forever.

I need to be forgiven for not being the person I used to be,

But most importantly, I need you to be open minded and patient with me. Show me a little empathy and understanding, even if you think I don't need it.

A grieving mother definitely needs a lot of things that almost no one can give them. Fathers do, too, but in a different way. For we are the ones who are connected to our baby from day one, not only with our hearts, but through the cord of life, from which we give our baby the nutrients they need to flourish.

We are not only their life line, but their protectors. Our wombs keep them securely nestled next to our hearts, which we surrender to them from day one. When our baby has to leave us before their lives ever start, it is a pain like no other.

And unless they've experienced it personally, no one knows what it's like to surrender their child into God's hands. So yes, we may need extra time even if it has to be 'til our breath leaves our bodies. You may think it's inappropriate to say their name at certain times of the year, but don't be. Our hearts can't be broken any more than they have been, but not acknowledging their lives, no matter how short, can truly damage our souls.

Do be courteous when announcing new pregnancies or births. It's not that we are not happy for you, but we, too, had wished this for ourselves at one time. It's true my life has changed. I am a shadow of the woman I once was, but it will be a long time before I get to cradle my baby in my arms, and sometimes that's just hard to accept. Love and hugs.

68

When a mother grieves, it's as timeless as her love.

Timeless, what a powerful and beautiful word to explain something so delicate. A word expressing how deep our grief runs, and how our love is forever strong for a child that left too soon. A mother's love for her children remains timeless, regardless of whether they out live us or we out live them. The love (and pain) we suffer through, every day, is never-ending, and becomes timeless in the way we hold their memories safe in our keeping. Never to be altered or forgotten - becoming timeless. As long as we remember and honor our angels' lives - then no one can ever say we had a time frame for how long we mourn. In a circle of love, we are bonded together forever with the precious life that now lives in Heaven. It is never-ending; it's timeless. Love and hugs, dear friends.

69

I found a beautiful and very moving picture of a statue. It is of a woman on her knees, resting her weary head in her left hand, which covers her sad face. She is draped over a small podium. She has on long skirts, and her head is covered in a lace shawl. And in her free hand that is hanging down the front of the podium, she holds a wreath of flowers.

Too often, we find ourselves in this same position when we visit our child's final resting place. I know I have, on many occasions, found myself crumpled down on my knees, sobbing uncontrollably. My heart is always laid bare and left very vulnerable to my internal grief. With my head in my hands, I cry out in hopes my Makaylee will not only hear, but feel, my love and longing for her. Even being consoled by my husband doesn't completely ease the tremendous longing to be with her. To have one more chance to feel love growing in my empty womb and the excitement of seeing her little face for the first time. But I know she hears my cries and feels my love for her in everything I do.

When I leave her, I know she feels my pain of separation even though she's been away from me for over fourteen years. So dear friends. if you need to weep. then sob. for there is nothing wrong with grieving the loss of your son or daughter. If you find yourself like this statue. whether it's at the graveside or in private, let your heartache be released. There are no boundaries for a broken heart - you're just showing your unconditional love, and there's nothing wrong with that. Love and hugs, dear friends.

70

I may talk, laugh and play my part

 But deep inside behind fake smiles

I have a broken heart.

I mourn for you deeper than anyone knows,

As the days go by my heartache grows.

Unfortunately, our lives will never be the same again. Our hearts will never stop hurting, and we will forever be caught in a world built around our brokenness. While others go about their daily lives, we will have to put on our masks of fake happiness to keep others at bay. We don't ask for outsiders' advice, because all we get is condescending remarks and unsympathetic looks. So, we do play our part the best way we know how. Finding others that are going through the same loss we are is a saving grace, because we can at least get empathy from true friends. We can at last pull off the masks we have to wear and show our true emotions, and broken hearts, without being judged. So, just remember you have friends here - no dress code required. Love and hugs.

71

My baby died.

Your advice is not needed.

I just need you to keep your comments to yourself,

Open your heart

And just take a walk with me

Until I can see colors again,

Not just black and white.

Most of the time this is how we feel, but we are too scared to tell our loved ones that this is what we need them to do. I know I've struggled with this several times after my daughter died. I finally came to the realization that I was the only one that would be keeping my daughter's memory alive. In times of grief, the majority of people see mourning only in black and white. When someone passes away, they are gone; you can't bring them back by crying all the time. That's grief in black and white. Well, news flash: we know this. It's not that we don't understand the way life works.

We know we can't pray or cry hard enough that God feels sorry for us and gives us our baby back. But we do see the world in black and white for a while, especially when we hurt so much. All aspects of life have no meaning to us, and we definitely don't need negative input from others who have no idea what it feels like to sing happy birthday to a headstone. It takes a while sometimes for us to see color again - just give us some time and a loving embrace, so we can handle our world without color.

Opening your mind to our depth of pain, even if only for a little while, will help us slowly add color back to our palettes, so we can survive life a little bit easier. But always remember, God will be here for us, and so will *Mothers of Angels*. Much love and hugs.

72

It takes an extreme amount of strength to love a child that you can no longer see, can never hold and will never hear, an invincible amount of strength.

When we see the word *invincible,* we tend to think of a super hero, someone who possesses such great strength and powers that nothing can destroy them. But for those of us that have to carry the burden of having to bury their own child, it puts us in that category. It takes an unimaginable amount of strength to have the will to carry on after such a tragedy. From the very moment our baby gains their wings, we, too, gain our super hero's cape and are given an invincible amount of strength, even though we don't feel it right off. A grieving parent, particularly the mother, has to develop this unimaginable power just to survive.

No other person can possibly fathom this amount of inner power that consumes a grieving mother, unless you've personally been through the same circumstances. It takes every fiber of our being to learn the uncertain terrain of our new path. Super hero powers are very much needed, but we can't be one of our many beloved characters of Marvel or DC. Instead, God gives us invincible strength to endure the remainder of our lives 'til we can be with our angels again. So, don't let anyone tell you that you are weak for mourning your child. Just remember that you are stronger than they think you are.

Not everyone can live this way in never-ending grief. It takes this special strength to make it day by day. We do, however, wear a very unique type of suit and cape, it's just not visible to those who haven't been through the death of a child. Love and hugs, my friends.

73

Envision a beautiful white marble sculpture depicting Jesus sitting down, and around him are children just clinging to him.

Dear Heavenly Father, could you do this for us;

MOTHERS OF ANGELS

Give our sweet babies hugs and kisses, your loving touch.

For we have been missing them so very badly, you see.

We would gladly do it ourselves, but it wasn't meant to be.

To gaze upon their sweet faces with love in your heart;

I know you'll tell them we never wanted to part.

But there's always a reason for the things you do.

We'll never understand why you needed our babies too.

We're forever grateful they'll never endure this life's troubles,

But while we are left behind without them, our heartache doubles.

All we wanted was to love and cuddle your precious gift

But all we have now are our memories of what if.

So until you see fit to call us home, we'll live through our grief.

By telling stories, embracing their trinkets and cling to our beliefs.

That you'll love our little ones 'til we get there;

Telling each one how much we care.

Thank you, heavenly Father, for doing this for us,

It's very important in you we trust.

Take our tears and turn them into love

And give them to our babies as kisses and hugs.

Amen.

74

No one will ever truly know the full extent of my love for you. After all, you are the only one who knows what my love sounds like from the inside.

Knowing that the main sound our baby heard was our heart beat is sometimes a very comforting thought. Our sons and daughters heard nothing but our unconditional love for them from the very moment they were conceived. No matter what was happening in the outside world, in the safe confinement of our womb, all they knew was pure love. However long they were with us, our babies could hear nothing but love coming from our hearts to theirs.

Now, even though they are no longer with us, I know they can still hear and feel our hearts beating with our undying love for them. I know the hurt my friends, but nothing will ever diminish how much we love and miss them. May your day be blessed, dear friends. Love and hugs.

75

I have come to realize that grief is similar to an earthquake. It's a natural occurrence where, at first, small trembles in the earth cause a disturbance noticeable by few. Then out of the blue, a big one hits leaving mass destruction in its wake. It is very hard to determine if the pieces that have been broken in its path will ever fit back together as they once did. And even if you manage to rebuild, there are still going to be aftershocks to remind us that life is never a guarantee or stability.

Our grief, anxiety and depression are truly similar to that of an earthquake. The initial event starts with the death of our child. When I was extubated from life support, I needed no one to tell me Makaylee had died, and even then, I did have warning signs of something not being right the morning of my tragedy. But for a lot of parents, there are no warning signs, and when it hits its readings are off the Richter scale. Everything you thought you knew and felt has now been forever altered. Just like the shifting tectonic plates that move unexpectedly under the many miles below our feet. The strong walls you happily built for your future, for your family, have now been cracked and damaged into practically nothing.

As time slowly creeps by, you try to patch your walls of grief and live a somewhat normal life. But just like any earthquake, we to have to prepare ourselves for aftershocks. Times when we are beyond words and hurting deep beyond the surface can be quite fragile for us and deepen the cracks in the walls of our heart. The walls we work so tirelessly to repair, just to help us survive without our baby, are by no means a solid foundation. It will always be unpredictable ground, and any little trigger can shake our emotions, causing a chain reaction. Grief is extremely unpredictable and will always have us watching the Richter scale for any changes. Love and hugs, my sweet friends.

76

Our baby was not just a feeling. They were a part of our lives. A very short and unpredictable part, but it also was just long enough to completely and forever change our lives.

As I sit here his afternoon and begin this post, I can't help but reflect on the last thirteen years and nine days. As I gather all the flowers, ribbon, and her tiara I find myself feeling anxious. In some ways, time has flown by so quickly while at the same time, it has completely stood still, as if she died only yesterday. Thirteen years ago, I had no idea how much my life was going to change in just nine short days. I reflect back on the wonderful naps that Makaylee and I shared after a hearty meal or how her father would always tell me our baby would be born sea sick due to all the rocking I did while watching television.

Reflection can be both good and bad in our recovery. It still amazes me that God blessed me with her, even if it was just for twenty weeks. In some ways, it felt like a lifetime, and even though I almost lost my life when God called her from my womb, I would gladly do it all over again. She changed my life in so many ways. Some were a blessing while others were a curse. No, it hasn't always been for the good, because I will be forever in mourning for the precious life that was taken from me. I have to say she was the better half of me, and that part of me died right alongside her on that fateful October morning.

But for five whole months, I was the happiest, most blessed mother on the face of the earth. So, I'll continue to gather my floral supplies and make the most beautiful birthday arrangement I can, in remembrance of the tiny life that made me a mother. It will be a very sad day, that I have no doubt but also a very beautiful day, as well. Love and hugs, my friends.

77

Bless the mother who has unwillingly lost a part of herself. She knows that her child is gone, yet she perseveres the only way she knows how. Never again will she see the reflection of the woman she used to be before her child departed, and it's hard for her to not feel cheated. The Bible says that you never give us more than we can handle, because you already know those of us who are strong enough to endure such a tragedy. But why, God? This task you have placed before her is a long, heartbreaking walk that sometimes she'll have to walk alone.

I pray that you lift her up higher than she has ever been, so she can withstand the waves of grief she will have to wade through. Catch her, each time she stumbles or falls, from speed bumps of mourning. Place angels in her path to soften some of the falls she will endure and to dry some of her tears. Keep her, as close to you as possible, within your loving embrace. Place a peace on her broken heart, for she'll need a constant friend.

78

Helpful pointers for helping the bereaved parent.

1. If they have other children please do not remind them to be grateful for them. They are aware of that blessing but having the baby they lost with them would mean so much more.

2. Never in a million years tell a grieving mother that she can always have more children. For some unknown reason, God has not seen fit to bless me with another child of my own. For us, the baby we lost was our only baby. And for those parents who are blessed enough to have more children, they are not trying to replace the one they lost.

3. For mothers like me, never tell us that maybe it was a blessing since we didn't actually get to meet our baby outside our womb. That's harsh and downright cruel, because we did know our babies from the very moment of confirmation of our pregnancy.

4. Do not ever tell us to get over it. The loss of our child is something that isn't taken lightly. The question that comes to mind would be,

which of your children could you lose and get over? It will never happen - accept that.

5. Do offer us a listening ear without condescending feedback, especially if you know nothing of our sadness.

6. Please talk to us about our child. Sure, we may shed some tears, but we would rather have you remember them with us than to act like they never existed.

7. And it would mean the world to us to receive a phone call, or just a card, letting us know that you are thinking about us on occasions like our child's birthday or the anniversary of their death. We don't want their life to seem in vain.

I know that the above statements are a bit bold and raw, but they are the truth, no sugar added. These are just a few ways that people in our lives can help in our grieving process.

We don't need to be dealt with; we are not a problem in society. So, don't ostracize us as if we were the plaque. We lost a child, and that child can never be replaced or forgotten. How could they be?

Sure, I know there are some people that don't care about the welfare of the precious child god blessed them with, but to those of us that had no choice in the way our gift was taken away from us, we care deeply about preserving what precious moments we had with them. I feel that the old saying, "If you can't say anything nice, then don't say anything at all," applies to statement.

For those who have been privileged to have their children outlive their parents, they have been blessed. But it doesn't mean we want advice from them on getting over our loss.

As I've learned, don't speak about things you know nothing about. Your child's memory, as well as my daughter's, will forever be remembered and cherished here. Love and hugs, dear friends.

79

A mother's unconditional love takes root long before her baby is born. It truly starts when she begins to dream of one day having a baby of her own. With those dreams, her natural instincts - that begin to implant themselves deep within the confines of her heart - include nurturing and love.

And regardless what some people think, a mother's love just doesn't go away when her baby dies. It never lessens or diminishes with time. If anything, her love for the child she carried, but now has to love from afar, will continue to grow stronger day by day.

As little girls, we dream of being a mother when we get our first baby doll. We naturally learn to hold, cuddle, feed and care for our baby dolls, and from that point on, we dream of the day we have one of our own. Some of us babysat while we were still in school. Now speaking from experience, babysitting can be a good wake up call to how hard it is to take care of a baby, but it also prepares us for motherhood.

I believe all women are born with some desire to have children, but not every woman is born to be a mother. There is a difference between the two, and proof of that can be seen every day on the news. That's why sometimes it is very hard for me to understand why my child died, when some women abuse, or even kill, their children. This will forever be one of life's biggest mysteries. As for those of us that have had to suffer the loss of a child that we had very much prayed for, we tend to frown upon the wrong doing of children by their parents. And we have every right to feel this way. For we have a love that rises above all the evil in this world. The mother who prays and yearns for motherhood only to have it taken away, has more love than most people will ever understand. The love and yearning we feel and suffer, as *mothers of angels,* will forever live on, only growing stronger with each passing moment. Love and hugs, my friends.

80

During our lives, we walk a lot of miles, and we always find our way home. But the absolute hardest and longest road we will ever have to walk is the one we are forced to walk after losing our baby.

The road we start to walk, to one day be reunited with our baby, becomes the absolute longest and most traitorous path. We are told that with time, the pain will ease and life will get better, but if anything, the pain becomes a constant companion, while life never changes. We often find ourselves yearning to be free from our life sentence and hold our sweet baby in our empty arms.

We want the road of broken hearts and unspent memories to stop making us walk on its unsteady and unforgiving road of sadness. Trying to keep the energy for life gets harder and harder, while the road we walk gets longer and longer. We use crutches along the way, but nothing will ever help us get us home faster.

But we have made some very supportive friends walking this lonely road. Some have been on this journey for a long time, while others have just begun. We have each other for support, so this road doesn't feel so lonely. *Mothers of Angels* boulevard now has forever-friends, and our walk won't seem quite as long or lonely. Love and hugs.

81

Always remember that certain dates or events will always trigger an emotional response. Birthdays, anniversaries, due dates and holidays will always be remembered and always be hard for us. So please be empathetic, and encourage communication when these times occur. It will mean more than you will ever know.

There is nothing more hurtful than when close family or friends fail to remember important dates that remind us of our baby. We understand, more than most, that for some people it is hard to talk about the baby that will never be, but for us, the parents, it is extremely hard to endure our sadness every day without every hearing a word of comfort or compassion.

But when special events like birthdays, or the anniversary of their death, we need to know that we are not the only ones thinking about the precious life that once was, then suddenly wasn't.

We are not asking for anyone to go into full mourning but it would be nice to hear a kind word of remembrance. We understand that you don't think about our angel every day because that's in our keeping, but please don't make us feel like their life, no matter how short or how long, doesn't matter. Acting like they never existed once they entered into God's hands doesn't make it easier on us.

It just makes us feel like you don't care. Like an "out of sight out of mind" mentality. But we see their image in our minds and hearts every day.

The smallest act of kindness could make the difference between us crying tears of sorrow or tears of anger. You wouldn't want your memory to fade out so quickly. Love and many hugs, dear friends.

82

The truth about the reality that people seem to place a "time frame" on is grief: Time does not and will never heal the wounds of child loss. All it does is put more space during your life to remember and relive your grief. Some wounds will never heal or stop hurting, no matter if the scar fades through time. They will always be there.

Time, how does one put a frame on this word? From childhood and as we grow up, we are told that with time things get better, change or get work out for the best. And in some circumstances, it does. But after Makaylee died, time no longer seemed to exist. In fact, it has become my heart's worst enemy, a constant reminder that every day is a day without my sweet angel. If anything, time stands still and seems to mock me. Lingering around, showing us what we are missing out on. Things that will never be, a life never lived.

It plays on our weakness to always remind us that our grief is only a heartbeat away. It has forever left a permanent scar, and one day, we will have an endless amount of precious time with the ones we had to let go of too soon. *One day* will become our friend and heal our scars, but until God reunites us, our love for our babies will continue to grow stronger with never-ending time. Love and hugs.

83

I've come to realize that grief is just love unfinished.

Unfinished, what a powerful word to use to describe the way we feel, each and every day spent without our little one. Grief can be so broad, but when it's explained as love unfinished, you really see a clear image of what we go through every day. We were blessed to start our journey of loving our little one, but sadly, they weren't meant to brighten this world, and therefore, their love resides in a better place. But for us, we didn't get to express the love we had instantly after we had confirmation of our good news. So, it is only fair to say our grief is love unfinished. We are left behind with empty arms and nowhere to finish our hearts' story. Unfinished becomes never ending. Much love and hugs, dear friends.

Displaying precious things around your house that remind you of your baby is not morbid or staying in grief. I have a memory box with a picture of Makaylee's last ultrasound, a copy of her footprints, a handmade bonnet made with tiny pink roses and lace, and the little pink angel rabbit the labor and delivery nurse gave to me. Beside her memory box is my sweet fur-baby Shyla's memorial. I have her picture in a frame along with a copy of her paw print. We had her cremated, and have her ashes in a small, beautiful urn.

When you walk into our home, you will see these precious things throughout our home. Some people would think I'm morbid, or just putting myself through more pain by seeing these things every day. But in truth, they comfort me. It's my way of keeping my baby's memories alive and honored. The way I see it, I will always be in mourning, but I will also not let the pain and suffering I endured, of losing both my babies, go in vain.

So, honor your little one the way you want to and as often as you want to. It is a part of healing, and if loved ones think otherwise, then maybe they shouldn't come over. Love and hugs.

84

We know that understanding our grief is very hard for others, especially loved ones. The extreme depths of sadness we have for our child can never be measured. A lot of times, even those who are close to us tend to forget how hard we mourn and they never will mourn.

Grieving the loss of my daughter has been the hardest thing I've ever had to endure. I've lost my mother when I was only five. due to suicide. And then suffered at the hands of an evil step-mother who found pleasure in beating a sickly child.

But I can honestly tell you that nothing has compared to having to bury my only child. I've always considered myself a somewhat strong person to have endured the hardships that life has thrown at me.

But losing my child that I had prayed for, and longed for, has definitely taken its toll on my heart. My emotions are always fighting a battle with reality, and it truly has been the hardest war I have ever had to fight. And it is an internal war that we, as mothers, struggle with the most.

Unless you have family or friends that have lost a child of their own, then they will never truly understand what we go through, just to survive, from one day to the next.

I have learned, from experience, that being an outsider to this life-changing event doesn't make you an expert in giving advice to those of us who are living it every day.

So please don't tell us how you would handle this type of heartache, especially if you've never been in our position. For those of us who are enduring our broken hearts every day, you are not alone. I know a lot of times it may feel like we are, and that is just one of the hard realizations we have to live with.

We are all struggling to survive - and just breathe. So, the friends we make here on *Mothers of Angels* will be the ones we can lean on for support and true understanding. Love and hugs, my friends.

85

I just wanted to take a moment and thank all of you who have opened your hearts and shared your amazing stories. Without all of you, this network of loving and caring people would have never been born. Every day, I look forward to sharing my heart with you and in return, I have gained many friends and know that if I need a listening ear, all I have to do is visit this page and read your kind words. Thank you for sharing your stories and allowing me to be there for each of you. I am extremely honored that all of you have joined this group, and I know God has truly blessed us beyond measure.

We are in this journey together, and I have a comforting peace knowing that we will forever be supportive of one another. God bless you all, my friends. Love and hugs.

86

Picture a heart, drawn in red, and not colored in. To one side of the heart is a pair of tiny footprints about the size of a Tylenol pill, and in the bottom corner is a phrase saying that there are just some holes that cannot be filled.

It's amazing how we think our life is so complete, and to some extent perfect, until we lose something so precious, like a child. My daughter, Makaylee, was the greatest gift I have ever been given. When she was called home, the hospital staff put together a little keepsake box that had her pictures after birth, and her tiny, perfect footprints safely tucked inside, for my keeping. For the longest time, I refused to open the tiny blue box, because I did not want reality to set in. But finally, I wanted to see what my daughter looked like and place my heart in there with what I had left of her existence. Her foot prints were the length of the tip of my pinky finger. They were so perfect and beautiful. My heart became hers in those moments. Coming from someone who was born with a hole in her heart, there is no greater emptiness left behind than the hole that's left after your child dies.

You find yourself trying to find patches to mend our broken hearts through prayer, counseling and good friends. Our children are supposed to be our living legacy, but when they are called home before us, we become theirs. Love and big hugs, my friends.

87

What people forget to realize is that whether our child is born or not; they always change our lives.

Remember when you were young and carefree. No worries or full knowledge of how hard life truly can be. Our minds were building a perfect world in which we would meet the man of our dreams, fall in love and get married.

With both of you working your dream jobs, you purchase that white picket fence dream house which your children will call home. Nothing but the perfect picture would do.

Finally, when we ventured out into the real world and began to achieve some of the dreams we had, we began to get relaxed, feeling like nothing could ever make our lives change. Then something unimaginable occurs. You find yourself facing the most horrible thing ever to happen.

You lose your child, and every dream you had seems to diminish and doesn't matter anymore. Even if you have more children, nothing can ever take the place of the baby you lost, and nothing will ever be behind that white picket fence. If you were to sit down and look back at the dream you laid out for yourself, you would now see a hole in that perfect life you had pictured in your mind.

Sure, your life has changed and you've adjusted, but when your baby dies, you have to completely learn how to survive, all over again. It's not an easy thing to do, and nobody will truly understand why, and you'll become a completely different person.

If you are blessed with other children, you will love them beyond measure, but there will always be emptiness in your heart where your angel baby will forever live.

And if you never get to have more children, you will carry all the memories of what might have been in your heart. Our children do change our lives.

We get to experience the good and the bad, but there will always be a broken fence that cannot be fixed. Keep the faith, my friends. Our fence will be mended one day. Love and hugs.

88

Many years ago, you had no idea that you would be here. You never knew that you would have to become extremely strong, like you are having to be now. Little did you know that you would develop a deeply rooted strength that would help you later in life. But you never gave up; you kept the faith that prepared you for the heartache you are facing right now.

Life rarely gives you a second chance to have something you so eagerly wanted. When we start making decisions on our own, too often we take the easy road and fall in love with others who handled their own missed opportunities, hoping to find the answer to our pain. Every now and then, we find ourselves at a crossroads, with no one in sight and a bundle of emotions that render us frozen in time. With each situation God puts us through, we learn new ways to handle our grief.

Slowly, we grow in our faith and realize that life is much more than we could ever imagine. When life throws a clot in your churn, you find out quickly how strong you are and thank God for all for the love, no matter what. Thanks to these events, we have learned to adjust to life's unpredictability, and we are so much stronger for it. Mourning a child is the hardest of these. It's a constant reminder that not all dreams come true, and how we stick together - as a unit - helps. So know this - we never walk alone. Love and hugs.

89

To understand life, we must find a common ground of being able to hold on and being able to let go.

MOTHERS OF ANGELS

It is easy for someone who has never had to endure the death of a child to tell those - that have - how they should get over it or move on. Having to let go of something you wanted, more than anything else, is hard enough, but to endure the emptiness a child leaves behind is unbearable.

Judgment from others is not required in order for us to know we must find a way to keep living, even when we feel like there is nothing to live for.

What more do people expect from us? Even though we had no choice in the matter, we still had to slowly accept letting go of our babies. But holding on to how we remember them is something that no one has the right to share their opinion on.

Unless you've had to stare at what might have been, then there is no possible way you could ever understand what it takes for us to let go.

Because every day we live without our baby is another day we have to let go. We are constantly reminded that *we* should be the mother in the department store picking out the things; *we* need to make sure our little one wants for nothing. Seeing the soft way she soothes her crying child back to sleep - forever haunts us.

Everywhere we look, it's like having life slap you in the face, and in a sly voice saying, *that will never be you.*

So please don't tell us what you would do, or how you would do it if you were in our shoes, because not everyone wears the same size. And forcing us to put on your shoes to move past the death of our child doesn't make you an expert in designing a more comfortable pair to "help" us move on.

I know for a fact that you could never wear the shoes I've been wearing, and mine will forever be too tight for you to handle. Love and hugs, sweet friends.

90

Any soul that has had to carry any form of empathy is a soul that has withstood an enormous amount of pain.

It is very hard for us, as parents to an angel, to comprehend that there are a lot of people who don't have empathy. You're not born with it. You learn the meaning of it through life experiences.

And even then, most people never truly grasp the concept of having empathy. Sure, they have sympathy, as we all do, but empathy is a whole other level of compassion that only happens when a tragic loss has been experienced.

The death of a child is, in my opinion, one of the hardest things that a parent could ever go through. Life has literally taken us to the darkest depths of sadness and left us there to blindly find our way out.

And only those who have been struggling out of that darkness will ever understand the importance of having and showing empathy to others just beginning their climb.

Living daily without our baby is hard enough to endure within ourselves, but its even harder when others can't open their hearts and minds to allow empathy and help us survive.

It is just sad, that in order for people to have this deep emotion, is for them to endure a life-altering reality. Just know that there is plenty of heartfelt empathy here for each and every one of you here. Much love and hugs.

91

I heard the absolute, most beautiful word said today. It was the sound of your name.

I couldn't tell you how often I think or say my daughter's name. Makaylee Denise. I was so excited when her father and I decided that this was the name our beautiful little miracle would be called. I found myself smiling every time her name was mentioned.

Her name became a household name, so to speak. After she died, it felt like everyone had forgotten the beautiful name of my daughter.

Through the years, I have learned that saying her name is my way of keeping her memory alive, and even though she is in heaven, hearing her beautiful name brings a smile to my heart.

Some people think that it's not healthy to say our angel's name, but I think it is very crucial for our recovery. The worst thing that people can do is never say their child's name.

The names we chose for our children mean something, and even though they are not physically here to claim it, it doesn't mean they don't want to hear it said. So say your child's name as much as you want, because I know they hear us and smile that we remember them. Love and hugs.

92

Not everybody will understand why we have trouble moving past the death of our child; they should praise God and count their blessings that they don't have to.

Every day we come across many people; some are family members and some are friends. Sometimes, it's just an acquaintance through social media who sometimes feels the need to criticize how we grieve our babies. Nine times out of ten they have never been where we are now, and unless they have lived through the death of a child, there is no possible way they could fathom what we endure from one day to the next. There is no moving past seeing the tiny, precious bundle of love, hopes and dreams, neatly placed in a casket, in which your whole world has been placed.

Unless you've sat at the graveside and stared at all that remains of your heart etched in stone, then you truly don't understand what we go through every second of every day. And we are glad that they haven't had to endure this kind of deep, gut wrenching pain. Nor would we ever wish it upon them. When someone voices their opinion on how we will one day move past this grief, don't hesitate to remind them how blessed they really are not having to endure such a tragedy. My friends, we are strong and firmly grounded in surviving this together. Everyone else's opinion need not apply. Much love and hugs, my friends.

93

Giving up is the easiest thing for anyone to do. Being able to keep going and hold it together, when everyone around us would completely understand if we fell apart, now that's nothing short of strength.

How *on-point* is this statement? Since becoming a mother to an angel, I have learned that parents who bury a child, whether it is one or more, are the absolutely strongest people I know. The heaviness we carry around 'til our last breath is the thickest air we will ever have to breathe. Not everyone could survive this kind of lifestyle we've had to adapt to. No, we're not always emotionally put together, but to choose to keep walking, on this never-ending, highly unpredictable road we've been forced to take, shows just how unbelievably strong we are.

God chose our babies for a reason. No, we don't understand why, and no, we never asked for this to happen to us. But God knew that we were firm in our faith in Him that no matter how dark the days got, our strength in our faith would see us through.

So, are we among some of the strongest people on earth - absolutely. Not everyone could handle loving and losing their child the way we have and continue moving forward. Love and hugs.

94

Please don't ever make the assumption that I am weak because I suffer from panic, anxiety and depression. You will never know the amount of strength it takes for me to just wake up every day and face the world.

When you lose a child, especially in a traumatic way, 99.9% of the time PTSD and anxiety take over every aspect of your life. When I was pregnant with Makaylee, we were told that due to my rare condition, having two uteruses, there was an extremely high risk to me and my unborn child. There were no guarantees that I would have a successful pregnancy, so therefore, the doctors and specialists had planned on delivering my daughter by c-section at seven months gestation. So, when I was starting my fifth month of pregnancy, I was feeling pretty confident that I would make it to seven months and have my whole lifetime to be a mother. Needless to say, I was caught completely off guard when the small uterus Makaylee was in ruptured at twenty weeks. It happened so quickly, and I had no control over what was happening to - or inside - my body.

One minute I was watching television, rocking in my glider rocker enjoying the thought of having my baby in a short few weeks, and then in the blink of an eye, I was fighting for my life, and my precious baby was gone. When you experience such physical pain, worrying about your baby and then waking up on life support, you are bound to be mentally scarred for life. It's 100% guaranteed that you will have flashbacks. So when someone tells you to just breathe when you have anxiety, remind them of the internal war you fight every second of every day.

We have absolutely no control over when it's an appropriate time for anxiety to consume every fiber of our being. It's just part of the war we continue to fight every day. Comments are not welcome or needed. Love and hugs.

95

No words can be found to help others understand just how stressful and hard it is to explain what's happening inside our hearts and minds. when we don't completely understand it ourselves.

When you lose a child, something inside you changes forever. Not only do you lose your baby, but a giant piece of your heart dies with them, leaving a gap so big that millions of uncontrollable emotions flow freely through, in, and around your broken heart. We are constantly tormented with "what if," "what could I have done," "why me," and many other questions on why our child had to leave. We are overcome with unpredictable and unwanted feelings of sadness and anxiety, even when our minds aren't solely focused on our child.

You have no control over when your heart decides to look for the baby that isn't in your arms, only to find emptiness. The human brain is a complex, super-absorbent sponge that never stops taking in any and all things related to our lives. When you add the death of a child, that sponge holds every ounce of grief, never letting one drop go.

It's a never-ending cycle which we will never understand, and it's even harder for outsiders to comprehend. But at least we have found one another and started something much needed in the world today, acceptance and understanding. I hope you all know *Mothers of Angels* is a God loving, open arms type of sponge. Everyone here shares the same brokenness of having something so precious taken away from us. We have a blessed group, and I know God has good things in store for us. Love and big hugs.

96

Almost everyone knows the look of admiration and love parents get when standing at the window of the maternity ward, pointing out their new arrival to family and friends. I often wonder if our children are gathered amongst the clouds looking down from heaven, having the same look of admiration and love while telling all the other children, "That's my mommy and daddy. Which one is yours?"

I always wanted to be able to experience this part of becoming a parent. I remember being extremely nervous and excited about getting to show off my beautiful daughter to all my family and friends, but sadly, that day never came. While I was fighting for my life, Makaylee's father had the honor of holding our precious baby and gazing upon her beautiful and perfect face. I have the pictures that my doctor took of her to look at when I want to see my little miracle, and God knows how proud I was, and still am, at being called her mother. There is no doubt in my mind that our little ones are looking down on us and showing one another whose parents are whose. We may have been cheated of showing off our bundle of joy, but while we cherish their memories, they are looking down on us, loving that we feel honored to be their mothers and they, our children. Love and hugs.

97

There is no such greater sorrow than to remember some happiness in those times of sadness.

As my daughter's birth and death date gets closer, I find myself thinking back on the short, but wonderful, time we had as mother and daughter. It's a bittersweet time of the year for me, and for thirteen and a half years, I had Shyla, my fur baby, to help soften the heartache. She always knew when I needed extra love and support.

We were truly connected, heart to heart. God sent her to me for that specific purpose, and now I will be mourning two precious angels. It is unbelievably hard to recall the happy and precious moments of our short time with our children, because they were called home before we were able to establish memories with them.

But that's the twisted part of being a parent of an angel. The bad always outweighs the good, and try as we may, recalling the moments of our happiness will always be with sorrow.

But if you find yourself thinking about all the little things that took place after getting confirmation of our pregnancy, don't hold back the smiles or tears. Those are your precious moments. Remembering them is the only way we can survive this life even if we have to smile with tears in our eyes to do so. Love and much hugs.

98

Our grief changes us; the pain left behind molds us into someone who feels more deeply. We come to cherish more openly. Tears flow more often and freely. Our hopes become desperate, but our love knows no boundaries.

I've known grief all my life, and I can honestly say that I have become more understanding, and have both empathy and sympathy, to others who have been grieving for many years, or just beginning their journey. But in doing so, I've also left plenty of room for hurt. If you were to think back before the death of your child, sure, your feelings were hurt a lot by everyday life and trivial things that with time, you learn from and move on. After you lose a child, your ability to block out and find a way to move forward with your life is virtually impossible.

The hurt that is experienced from a psychological perspective is far too deep to just simply "move on." For those of you who have been blessed with other children after the loss of a child, I have no doubt that you appreciate every second with them. Even when they are driving you crazy, I know that you think back on the little one you lost and you feel blessed that God gave you another chance to experience parenthood.

Grief has definitely left me crying. Downright sobbing, to be honest - every time I watch the news you can bet there will be a 50/50 chance of hearing a story of child abuse or child neglect and death. Nine times out of ten the parent is responsible, and that just fuels the fire of my grief. I cry for the child lost. Having hope, as we walk this path of grief, becomes crucial to our survival. 'Til this day, I still desperately hope to be blessed with another child, even though I know it will never be.

You never lose hope for all the things you've missed out on. And lastly, even though the loss of my only child has left me forever broken hearted, I still manage to love more deeply. It's crazy when you think about it. To have such an emptiness in our hearts after losing the most precious part of ourselves, only to find we can still love more deeply than most people we know, is truly a testament of our faith. Only God could give us this ability, because most people would not blame us if we became bitter and shut off. But our heavenly Father made us better than that.

So yes, grief has definitely changed us, even if the thing we want most of all can never be given back. Much love and hugs.

99

You will soon know to not become angry or aggravated with a woman who is mourning the death of her child, because she is battling with demons far greater than you may ever comprehend.

As a parent who has lost a child, have you ever had someone ask why you still think about your baby? I know I have, and each time a comment was said in negativity regarding my daughter, I found myself feeling a rage building within my soul that could trump the devils.

It felt like being sucker-punched in the face by the people who I thought were my support system. For those who have never had to let go of a child that they loved, and wanted more than anything else in this world, they know absolutely nothing about the inner demons we fight.

The thoughts and feelings we go through forever keep us struggling to breathe. It takes everything we have, just to survive the pain and heartache we feel every time we see others living life with their children. Having the experiences and making the memories we deserve to have with our little one.

So, yes, we still think about our children and what they would look like, or what they would be doing even after months and years go by. So please don't act surprised or concerned about our well-being when we reminisce about the child that was ripped away from our hearts. Love and hugs.

100

One of the hardest questions asked is, "how many children do you have?"

I could not tell you how many times I have been asked this question. More than I can count, I know, and every time, it tears a piece of my soul and pushes the air from my lungs. But I can honestly say, without any hesitation, that I have always answered one and she is in heaven. Just because she's physically not here doesn't mean that she isn't in my heart. With agonizing pain in my heart, I tell them that my daughter passed away almost fourteen years ago.

Some people would say that technically, I have no child, but they are wrong. She did live, if only for twenty weeks, and she lives on within my heart.

I know that asking how many children one has is a natural question, because in a semi perfect world, the majority of people have children. We are raised with the understanding that the cycle of life usually goes as follows: you're born, you grow up, get married and have children of your own. But for those of us who have lost a child, whether God blessed us with other children or just with the one he took back, this age-old question still stings us to our very core. I've started telling everyone that I do have a daughter but God saw fit to have her born into his keeping. Never be too broken to answer this question when asked. Proudly say your baby's name, because even though my Makaylee is physically not here to claim her name, she lives on inside me.

But having said that, the heartache of being asked this question does make me very sad, and I sometimes wish people wouldn't ask. but in some way, that's how I make sure her life, no matter how short it was, will forever be remembered. So say their name, and take pride in being a mother to an angel. Love and hugs, sweet friends.

101

All you ever hear about is how painful child birth is, but to me, there is no greater pain than having to bury one.

I have never experienced the physical pains of giving birth. Nature has made that a harsh reality. I did however, witness natural child birth while I was in nursing school. Before you graduate, you have to go through clinicals in each department of a hospital, to show you have experienced the many stages of life from birth to death.

Of course, before you observe any medical procedures, you have to have the patient's consent. During my maternity rotation, a woman came to the hospital in very active labor.

I was already dreading this part of my training, but I asked the mother-to-be if I could observe her child being born, and she gladly welcomed me. She had already had three other children, so she was no stranger to the birthing process. I, on the other hand, had no clue what to expect, and instead of the mother being anxious and scared, I held that place for her.

In a matter of minutes, I witnessed one of the most amazing parts of life. As the woman did her labored breathing and pushed when she contracted, I watched as her son came into this world.

With all the tears I was crying, you would have thought that *I* had just given birth while *everyone else* looked on. My emotions were all over the place, because I finally got to see what I had missed out on with my own daughter. Seeing this beautiful miracle unfold, before my eyes, was a harsh reminder that I would never get to experience this wonderful part of life. Watching the mother holding her newborn was truly a magical experience, and I did ask her if the pains of childbirth go away once she got to hold her baby. She told me that it was the best feeling in the world, but that you never really forget the physical pains. That your body endures, but having a healthy child in your arms definitely suppressed it. And it must, because what I saw and heard that day while that tiny life was coming into this world, I would not blame any woman from stopping at just one baby.

But for those of us that have had to bury a baby, not getting to reap the benefits of motherhood, the pain is much greater than any contraction. We are left with empty arms and a broken heart, and to me, this type of pain is much greater than any form of giving birth. For the mothers that are blessed with the fruits of their labor, we are left with only memories, and most of the time, that just makes it worse. So, until you have had to endure the heart break of having to look at a headstone with your child's name etched into it, then you have no idea just how deep my pain truly goes. Love and hugs, dear friends.

102

If you truly looked at me, you would see that I am not the same person I used to be. Everything has changed; it had to. So please don't expect the same person to be in the present, because she no longer exists. For who you see now is a shadow of the past, and that part of me is no longer who I am.

It's no secret that our lives are forever changed by the passing of our child. From the very second they left us here, we had no choice but to be changed. It's a part of our flight or fight response. A part of us wants to run away from the reality of living every day without our baby.

Having to feel the endless emptiness in our hearts, that comes with burying a child, is almost unbearable.

The other part of us remains in a constant battle to keep what precious memories we do have with our babies alive and forever in our thoughts, no matter the tears we shed in mourning. We are no longer the person people remember, but a deeply, forever changed soul. Lost but still here; wandering endlessly through life with a massive scar on our hearts that only we can feel.

Being a mother to an angel is an extremely difficult burden to bear, but the love we have for our babies will never truly die while we are living. God has them in His keeping for now; we have them in our hearts. Love and hugs.

103

There are those who come through a traumatic experience and are able to talk about it. Others have the ability to just act like it never happened and just never talk about it. Some people find interesting ways of expressing their grief, while others just feel lost. Everybody copes with tragedy in their own unique ways, and that's okay. So if you ever find yourself looking at someone else's life and think that they have it all figured out, just remember… you may not want to be in that person's position just because they seem unbothered by things around them. They may look like a calm ocean, but know that the ocean has no boundaries. And while in some parts that person may be floating on calm waters, in others, they may be sinking.

There is absolutely no wrong way to grieve the loss of a child. It's a path that only you can decide to take. But no matter which path you take, beware there will always be someone waiting along the way to throw criticism and unwanted advice on your path.

I remember my grandmother, my biological mother's mother, telling me that in her day, mentioning a pregnancy, much less a loss of one, was considered a very private affair and should never be talked about outside closed doors. So when a miscarriage occurred, you were expected to be the dutiful wife, hide your sorrow from the outside world even to your husband, and continue on with everyday life with an excellently crafted mask placed over your pain and continue as if nothing ever happened. Through the years, some mothers have removed their masks and turned their grief into something to help others, or to help take their minds off the emptiness they feel inside.

Some feel led to adopt or foster a child in need of a loving family while mothers like me write a book about their loss and start a support group for parents who just don't know what to do. I hope to break the cycle of keeping a closed mouth policy on child loss. No matter how a grieving parent decides to handle their pain, there is no right or wrong way to mourn. No extra judgment is required, especially if you've never chartered this type of stormy sea.

Our ocean of grief runs far and very deep. It never stays the same on - or under - the surface. But push us too far, and you may find yourself in uncharted waters, trying to out run a tsunami bigger than any natural disaster ever created. So, my friends, grieve how you see fit. No one has the right to sail in your sea of heartache and tell you how to ride out the storms. You've earned the right to be shown the respect any ocean demands.

Whether it's floating on calm waters or barely treading the choppy waves, you grieve your child how you want to; if others want to row the boat and judge, then put them in a life boat and send them on their way. I hope everyone has some smooth sailing today. Love and hugs, my friends.

104

For any mother who has endured child loss, I can tell you she feels defeated and weak as she mourns the harsh reality that there was absolutely nothing she could do to save her child. All she could do was watch helplessly as death robbed her of her happiness.

How helpless I remember feeling, the whole time I was fighting for my life, knowing that my baby would only survive if I did. I vividly remember trying, ever so hard, to fight the overwhelming urge to just give up and close my eyes in order for the excruciating physical pain to stop. The demands of my body urged me to stop fighting, because it had passed the point of no return.

In my mind, as I went in and out of consciousness, I believed my unborn child would still have a chance if I just fought the darkness off long enough. I'm a natural born fighter - since the day I was brought into this world. Being born premature and with heart disease, I was only given a four percent survival rate my first night of life.

So knowing I defied the odds, I just knew my daughter would be the same way.

But after I woke up on life support, with tubes and pumps connected to almost every part of my body, I instantly knew that my precious Makaylee was no more. My earthly body had failed me and her both. Over time, I have realized that there was absolutely nothing that could be done to save my baby, but it doesn't stop me from enduring survivor's guilt.

And just like all of you, we will never know the true reasoning why God took our babies back. But I do know that she is safe and sound just waiting on me to join her when I am called home.

Sure, I feel helpless every day when I have anxiety, or have a flashback on the events that took my daughter's life and almost mine, and sadly, that will never go away.

That's just life. But knowing we will see them again, and never have to worry about going through another painful separation, is reassuring. And we will never have to worry about fighting to protect them ever again. Love and hugs.

105

God called your name so gently that only you could hear. No one heard the footsteps of the angels drawing near. Softly from the shadows, there came a gentle call, you closed your eyes and went to sleep, you quietly left us all. Author: unknown

This just spoke to me. I can just hear God's sweet, soothing voice calling out Makaylee's name in the early morning hours of October 26th. What a beautiful way of describing our babies ascend into God's loving embrace. I can envision a beautiful angel being at our side the whole time we are carrying our sweet little one. Placing a comforting hand on our wombs, gently soothing our baby to a peaceful sleep, and what a beautiful sight awaited them when they opened their eyes.

I can only imagine the angel that so carefully cradled my Makaylee, so lovingly in her arms, stepping into Heaven to the waiting family members that have gone on before us. But not before the angel ever so gently placed a loving kiss on her forehead to wake her up, while placing her in God's loving embrace. And just as quickly and quietly as our baby came into our lives, they left us just the same. I can't imagine it any other way. Such a beautiful transition - and that's where they will patiently be waiting for our loving embrace when our angel carries us home to God's sweet grace, never to part, ever again. Love and hugs, my friends.

106

Only until you've gone through child loss will you ever know what it feels like to feel sad, every single day, even when there are times of joy.

Sometimes it is hard to believe that I am living this life without my daughter. Having tearful moments more than any other time in my life, I can honestly say I never thought I would cry for so many years and know that I'll be crying for many more to come. As mothers to angels, none of us expected to always carry tears, even on the best of days.

I've missed out on so much that most parents make memories from.

When I earned my nursing degree and my first book was published, I would have given anything for Makaylee to be here to celebrate these accomplishments with me. Even though my book is based on her, it would have been written as a tribute to defeating the odds and having the happy ending I so desperately wanted. Not about the tragic heartbreak I endured from her death, and living the memory of what might have been.

For every birthday, holiday and family gathering that have been spent in silence and wishing that you could just disappear. All of our moments have changed forever; whether good or bad, our hearts bear the sadness we have to so gallantly hide. Having a broken heart from losing a child forever stays with us, and nothing we do or say will ever change that. We just have to paint the smile on our face and start each day the best way we know how. Even if the tears aren't streaming from our eyes, it doesn't mean that they aren't pouring from our hearts. Love and much hugs, my friends.

107

Tears are very unique; they are not necessarily a sign of weakness. They can speak volumes of strength, happiness or the amount of unconditional love we feel. They become tiny messengers and reminders of what we've loved and lost.

Our tears represent many forms of our emotions. The obvious types of tears are non-verbal ways of showing sorrow. Some people cry out of frustration or in times of imminent anger. We find ourselves crying uncontrollably when we think about our baby, who had to leave us way to soon. Sometimes we cry out of frustration that we have been robbed of our child, and of the many hopes and dreams we will never get to have.

Our tears are really an eloquent way to show our love, not our weakness. When we are at our lowest point of grief, which we will find ourselves in that place quite frequently, we have a multitude of tears that stream down our faces, clearly showing how broken we feel, but also how immensely strong we are. Having to live each day with a broken heart is not an easy way to live but for us. We have no choice but to cry when we need to, and sob when necessary. Never underestimate our tears of sorrow for a moment of weakness to take advantage of our pain. We may look weak and broken, but have no doubt, whatsoever, that we are stronger than the average parent.

In truth, we love deeper, and suffer our loss with the utmost respect for those who see us in our time of mourning. Love and hugs.

108

A simple pink rose, still partially closed, with the fresh dew of morning laid gently on each petal like a soft touch. That's how beautiful you are in my heart for all eternity.

I cannot wrap my mind around the cruel fact that this day, fourteen years ago, would be our last together. Never in a million lifetimes would I ever think that this day would forever change my life and take yours. Sometimes it feels like it was just yesterday that I was rocking you, while you slept soundly inside my womb. All the worries I had were those of keeping you safe until you were developed enough to make your entrance into this world.

I know technically you didn't die until the early hours of the 26th of October, but today, the 25th, is the hardest for me, because all I remember is the horrible way you left this world.

And now that Shyla is with you in Heaven, I find myself beyond sorrow because when she was here, I still had a piece of you with me, and she knew that. Tomorrow, I will bring both of you a birthday arrangement to celebrate your lives, so until then, just know Mommy loves you both so very much, and every day without you is a day without air. Love and big hugs.

109

I've had some people say, "I don't know how you do it. Endure the pain of burying a child," and I tell them that I never really had a choice.

My friends, today is the day that I hate the most. In the early morning hours fourteen years ago, I had finally succumbed to the demands of my tired body and was placed on life support in order for my doctor to perform an emergency c-section and hopefully save my life. My chances were growing slimmer by the second, and my sweet Makaylee was already gone.

While I was fighting for my life, my baby girl gained her wings and didn't leave me mine. Over the next few hours, I would be getting multiple blood transfusions, IV antibiotics and fluids to help heal my damaged body, while a machine kept me alive. My family and friends sat helplessly in the waiting room, saying prayers for my recovery. When I finally opened my eyes again, I could feel the air being forced into my lungs and hear my brain screaming that something very bad had happened.

I do, however, recall instinctively knowing that my baby was gone. Even as I fought against the restraints, I also was praying that God would not let me draw breath ever again. I wanted to be off life support so I could just die. From the moment I opened my eyes for the first time in my in my new life, I so desperately prayed to be taken from it, because a piece of my heart and the better half of me left with my Makaylee. But God had other plans in store for me, and fourteen years later, I'm not always 100% sure I've found that purpose. But I did write *My Heart Shaped Womb* with the thought of helping others have some hope for survival after the horrific tragedy of child loss.

And in doing so, I made sure Makaylee's life stays alive through me. I have been asked how I keep going on after everything I've been through, and I'll tell you it's not easy by a long shot. Mourning my daughter has been my greatest challenge yet, and I know I will always be in a state of grief until my dying day.

I've learned that, in order to survive this and have some sense of purpose, I have to take a second-by-second type of approach. So this afternoon, I will place the flower arrangements on the monuments marking both my babies' final resting place in celebration of their life and death. We can only play the cards we've been dealt, sweet friends, even though we wish for the one card that would make us have the winning hand. Much love and hugs.

110

Be careful not to tell a grieving mother that her child is in a much better place, because for her, the best place for her child is cradled in her arms.

As I sit here reflecting on the day we laid Makaylee to rest, I remember hearing several people say these exact words to me. I never needed anyone to tell me my daughter was in a better place. In this world we live in, I find myself grateful that she doesn't have to endure the evils of this world, but it doesn't take the yearning of wanting her here with me. I want nothing more than to have my daughter here with me so I could hug her, see her, touch her and tell her how much I love her. And to be able to tell her that there was no greater gift given to me than her being mine. But for whatever reason, God saw fit to have her join him in the safest most sacred place, where one day I'll be with her again. So yes, she is in a better place. But as her mother, who was left behind, I would rather have her safely nestled in my arms. Love and hugs 'til tomorrow.

111

Recognizing signs of grief

- Crying all the time and not really knowing why

- Missing the one you lost, uncontrollably

- Feeling like you are the only one grieving

- That no one else understands what you're going through or feeling

- Longing to talk to the one you lost

- Longing to go back to the way things used to be

- Trying to figure out if you did something wrong or if there was anything you could have done differently.

Being a grieving parent, we know all these feelings, all too well. It's become our way of life. I know that I find myself completely at my heart's mercy when I feel the twinge of heartache grip me, and all I can do is cry. When someone asks us to describe how much we miss our little one, sometimes there are no words that could possibly explain our sorrow.

I know we often feel like no one in the entire world could possibly know what we are struggling through. We feel isolated and singled out. We long to hear the little heartbeats, or the soft cry of our baby, to wake us from this nightmare. Begging God to make us numb to the hurt that never seems to ease, and we sometimes find ourselves willing to do anything to re-do the tragedy we have to endure. Know that everyone here feels all of these things, every second of every day. God sent you here for a reason. You are never alone, my friend. Love and hugs.

112

An artist by the name of Celeste Roberge created a very moving sculpture titled "The Weight of Grief." It is the form of a human being made out of thick wire. The artist made the body crumpled down on their knees in a crouched position. To emphasize the indescribable way grief is, different shaped and sized rocks were placed inside the wire frame. If you can look it up, please do, because it is absolutely a breathtaking work of art.

This artist captured the true essence of what we feel every second of every day. The various shapes and sizes of rocks used truly shows the different depths of depression and anxiety we carry after the death of our child. If someone were to ask me how it felt to bury a child, I would show them this sculpture.

Finally, someone found a beautiful and accurate way to show our way of life. How the body is completely crumpled to the ground in agony, and you can see the weight of sadness and despair holding the human spirit down. I could not have made anything that accurately depicts the true nature of what we endure. Just remember, my friends; you are not carrying your loss by yourself. *Mothers of Angels* is sharing the weight of loss with you, always. Love and hugs.

113

In a lot of ways, grief is like glitter. When you throw some up in the air, it scatters all over the ground. But when you try to clean it up, you never truly seem to get it all. In fact, you will never be able to find each piece in order to throw it away. Bits and pieces of glitter will remain hidden in the smallest of cracks and crevices that you never knew were there. And just like grief, glitter will always be somewhere, *always.*

Grief is a lot like that piece of glitter that you keep finding every time you sweep your floors. That one piece somehow multiplies no matter how often we vacuum, sweep or mop. Grief is the same way, in that it doesn't matter what you do to help ease the amount of pain it causes, there will always be more hiding just around the corner. I know when I make Makaylee's flower arrangements, I often use ribbon that has glitter on it, and when making bows and repositioning flowers around to make it look just perfect, I get glitter everywhere.

When I sweep my floors, I always have a small amount of glitter still shimmering in the dust pan. I manage to find pieces of shiny pink or purple for months after I've taken the arrangement to the cemetery. Grief, anxiety and depression are the same way. Just because you get help in managing your sorrow, there will always be little reminders that appear in your memory, bringing back the heartache you have tried so hard to keep suppressed.

And I'm not saying that hiding these feelings is what we need to do. I highly recommend acknowledging them. Just like glitter, our loss will always be with us. It will always hide in corners and crevices of our hearts and minds, just waiting to be swept out. No amount of counseling will ever completely rid our lives from the grief we feel when we lose a child. It does, however, help us learn to survive the shattered pieces left behind, so we can have some hope of life after loss. We will always see or find something that reminds us of what we've lost. But just like glitter, the memory of our little angel will forever be with us.

Many years from now we will find little specks of the glitter that is our grief. It will bring tears to our eyes, but be grateful that you still have those beautiful, precious pieces to remind you of the baby you once had - the honor of being a parent, too. It just means they will forever be with us. Love and hugs, my friends.

114

When a baby dies, it's easy for people to say that God needed another angel, but He didn't ask them for their child.

During Makaylee's funeral, it was said that God sometimes needs little angels to help brighten up heaven. Well, I'm two-sided on this. On one hand, I feel truly honored that God chose my precious daughter to help show love and happiness to loved ones that have gone home before us. I mean, who else is going to help God paint his beautiful sunsets?

On the other hand, I do wonder why my child had to be the one chosen for this purpose. Sometimes, I feel cheated and upset, especially when her birthday - or Mother's Day - comes around, and all I have to feel like a mother are the bright beautiful colors that accompany the sun as it sets. It's only human nature to have these feelings. But I have to remember that God has a perfect plan for my life, and he placed Makaylee in that plan at just the right time. I will never fully understand what my purpose in this world is, but I do know my daughter strengthened my walk with God and gave me the promise of seeing her again.

And I know this, because of the out-of-body experience I had while I was fighting for my life. All I remember was being in a very peaceful place with a bright white light shining all around me. I could see the doctors and nurses, frantically working to save my life, while my dying body lay on the operating table. I saw all the tubes and hoses going in and coming out of my worn-out body, but I heard nothing except peaceful silence. I had no doubt that I was in the presence of my lord and savior. And that's all the reassurance I need of our reunion.

So, when someone says that Heaven needed another angel in regards to your precious baby, remember to just breathe and smile, because even though they have no idea how bad those sweet words hurt, it may be their way of saying something they feel is worthy of your child's honor. Love and big hugs, my friends.

115

Close your eyes and imagine yourself ever so tenderly holding your sweet baby with their tiny wings folded on their backs. One arm firmly holds our angel close to us, while the other hand gently caresses their little head against the nape of our neck. How precious this vision is to behold.

When you can imagine this beautiful moment, you really get the true essence of the love a mother has for her child. The sweetness of the way she cradles her baby, even though she knows she can't keep the precious angel God bestowed upon her. This is how a lot of you had to say goodbye to your baby. I sometimes wish that God would have allowed me to hold my Makaylee, if only for a little, while before I had to let her go.

I never had the chance to even lay eyes on my beautiful baby girl, but I can only imagine that this would be the way I would have embraced her. To be able to physically connect with her, before she was taken from my world. I have no doubt that each one of our babies could feel our loving embrace as they entered into the gates of Heaven. Our bond and unconditional love is living proof of that. Love and hugs, my friends, love and hugs.

116

Dear Mommy, I never really went anywhere. I just left your womb and entered your heart.

This is a beautiful way of remembering our baby, isn't it, because that's exactly what took place when they passed. From the very moment they left our wombs, they left their love and precious memories imprinted on our hearts, so we wouldn't feel so empty every time we thought of them.

Some people would probably think we wouldn't have anything, really, to remember of a baby that never was born. But if anything, we have the most to remember. The memories we hold in our hearts is the only place they can't be taken away or forgotten. So while others continue to make memories, ours are forever frozen in time - so to speak. Safely tucked away in the warmest place God made, our hearts. And while we still have breath in our bodies, and no matter how broken our hearts feel, our babies will live on.

Every time you feel a twinge of sadness pump through your heart, that's just a gentle reminder of our sweet angel's existence. Love never dies even, after we die. Therefore, the memories and love we carry for our child, and their love for us, will forever live on in the confines of our hearts. Much love and hugs.

117

A distinctive type of pain comes from getting your heart prepared for a baby that will never be.

In our lifetime, we lose so many family members and friends that leave us with heartache and the pain of having to say goodbye. But speaking from a whole life of experience on both sides, the death of my only child has definitely been the hardest thing to endure. I lost my mother, at the age of five, to suicide, a close friend in a car accident in high school and multiple grandparents, all before I turned twenty-five.

From the moment I heard my baby's heart beat for the very first time, I feel in love. My heart was utterly and completely consumed with unconditional love for the precious life that was growing inside me. As they say, I was over the moon. I never knew how much love you could have for someone you never met, and wouldn't meet, for at least forty weeks.

You become co consumed with the unlimited possibilities of the beautiful future you envision for your precious little one. Until God has other plans, and your little one becomes an angel. Then, and only then, do you feel the gigantic hole left from all the great dreams you had, and no place for all the for all the love to go that we have for our baby. But I have no doubt that God shows them every day how much we love and miss them by filling their hearts with our love. A love that lasts a million times longer than a lifetime. Love and hugs, sweet friends.

118

When I open up to you about my child, I don't want you to feel pity for me, and I definitely don't want you to feel sorry for me. I tell you because I need for you to understand exactly why I've become who I am.

For those of you who have read my first book, *My Heart Shaped Womb,* you know that from childhood, my life has been a never-ending battle of survival. When I decided to share my life's story with the world, it took a lot of praying and pondering, because my life is nothing for the faint of heart. While writing it, I decided to not sugarcoat the ugly parts, because I wanted people who have suffered through the same things I had to finally feel that they were not alone.

I have never wanted anyone to feel sorry for me, but I do want some respect for what I've overcome. The things that happened to me prior to Makaylee's death, and after, have made me who I am today. Am I still the same person I was growing up? Absolutely not. Everything that I've been through has made me a stronger Christian woman who has a solid testimony of how God has worked in my life.

Do I wish that I had a different outcome to some of the misfortunes I've had, like the death of my child? Absolutely. I still wish she was here with me. I would give anything to have her back; what parent wouldn't? But for some reason, God chose her to be mine only for a short time.

Never let others think that you are weak because you grieve for your child. We are stronger people for it. Together we are like a band of superheroes in our own right. I hope everyone has a blessed day. Much love and hugs.

119

What makes an angel mom? It's when you have held life in your womb, if only for a short time, or for the full term of nine months. When your baby's life ended, either inside your womb or after birth, you instantly become a mother to an angel. Some of us get to meet our baby and have them for years; some meet their baby too soon, while others never lay eyes on the beautiful child God gave to us.

Angel mothers are the strongest most incredible beings I know, because it takes an extreme amount of strength and courage to endure such heartache and continue moving forward. Courage is her name.

This position of parenthood we've been handed is extremely hard and never rewarding. We never get to delight in the joys that other parents get to, and for those of you who have the added blessing of other children; there is still an empty void that will never be filled.

Whether we get to visibly see and hold our baby, if only for a moment, or if we never get the chance to do either, the love we have for our baby does nothing but grow stronger. The extreme amount of strength we have in giving up our babies takes an immense amount of love, like no other we will experience. To want and pray for a child so badly, being blessed with finally conceiving our miracle child, planning and having great dreams for a happy future, only to unwillingly have it ripped away in a blink of an eye. It is a pain far greater than most people will ever have to endure or understand in their lifetime.

The constant reminders in everyday life that plague our hearts of things we will miss out on. The never-ending battle of trying to keep our sanity from leaving us just like our child did - it takes an unfathomable amount of strength to be a mother to a child that has angel wings. Much love and hugs, my dear friends.

120

I found a beautiful drawing of Jesus holding two newborn babies in his arms, and the peaceful and loving look on his face is so serene.

The hymn "He's Got the Whole World in His Hands," well, He truly does. My Makaylee was my whole world, just like your baby was yours. This is a priceless picture that captures the beauty of Jesus's love for our children, and the knowledge that they are in the safest hands besides our own. The heartwarming way he is looking upon them brings some comfort to my heart.

I know that this would be the same exact way I would have gazed upon my daughter's face if God had chosen to let her live. Even though my whole world has been in Heaven for fourteen years, it doesn't make the pain of missing her any less. And while I know that she is being loved and cared for by the best, I can't wait to meet her with open arms and a full heart again. Then, and only then, will I have my whole world in my hands.

Until then, I know she is very well taken care of by God, family members and friends that are already there, just waiting on us to join them. Blessings, love and hugs.

121

Even as you were born still, no cries of life passed through your tiny lips. Your eyes never saw the light of this world; we never saw one another. I never felt your tiny fingers wrap around one of my fingers, and you never reached out to touch my face or to be picked up. The sound of your voice will never be heard, and the sweet smell of your skin will never linger in our memories.

Why did death rob me of all these precious things? Why couldn't we have just given you the breath of our lives to sustain yours? You will always be my forever story that will never have fulfilled pages of memories. I will always speak your name, because you will remain the most precious life that never got to live. Born, but not born.

When I finally looked at the pictures of my Makaylee that my doctor had kindly taken so I could see my baby, she was absolutely the most beautiful angel of perfection I had ever seen. Ten fingers, ten toes. The most beautiful face I had ever laid eyes on. She had her daddy's full lips, and I can't imagine what color her eyes were, but I bet they would have melted hearts.

She was so tiny and perfect. At the time, it still felt like a bad dream that the beautiful baby in the pictures I held in my hands was no longer in my womb, growing and thriving, just waiting to make her debut into this world. I have no doubt that she would have had both her father and me wrapped around her little finger from day one. She already had our hearts.

I remember just sitting there staring at the pictures, waiting for her to breathe or move. My mind knew that she never would, but my heart was much harder to convince, still is, most days. As we get older, death becomes less of a surprise and more of a reality, but when we are young and starting families of our own, the death of a child seems so impossible and unrealistic. We don't think God will take a new, innocent life before it has started, and yet for us, we know all too well that death knows no age. It has no limitations or discriminations. Nor does it have a set time frame on how long we stay on this Earth, living to be a hundred or dying while in the womb.

My Makaylee will always be beautiful and perfect, no matter how old I live to be, and death can never take that away from me. She lives on forever in my heart, the most precious baby I've ever seen. Love and hugs.

122

How to show support for grieving parents:

- Always provide a safe and loving environment.

MOTHERS OF ANGELS

- Please don't try to "fix" our pain.

- Try to understand that this is NOT about you.

- Know that our sorrow will be unpredictable.

- Please just be honest if you're uncomfortable or unsure of what to say.

- Don't say things that can be hurtful.

Explaining ways that loved ones can help us live through our grief is sometimes very hard to do. I found this list to be somewhat helpful while doing some research. Having a safe place for us just to be able to go to, and not be ridiculed or judged for the way we mourn our child, is very important.

We don't need anyone to fix our pain, because there is absolutely nothing that can be done to bring them back. Trust me; we have tried everything humanly possible already. Counseling, and sometimes medication, can help ease the symptoms of our grief, but no matter what we do, our broken heart will always be waiting on us. When we have a breakdown, we don't need others to lessen our pain by saying things like, *this happens every day all over the world.* That doesn't mean anything to us when we are hurting. We are not concerned about what others think about our ways of grief.

We know how bad things happen to good people all the time; we are living proof of that. When we need a shoulder to cry on, just be there. We also don't need comments on how you would handle our situation if you were in our shoes. Be aware that our sadness will forever come in waves. Any little thing can cause us anxiety and push our depression deeper. Sometimes when we don't attend certain events, it's not because we don't love and care for you. It's because we have to protect ourselves from situations that trigger our memories of what we can't have.

And please remember the golden rule; if you can't say anything nice, then don't say anything at all. Sometimes silence is the best support anyone can give. And lastly, sometimes hearing our loved ones say that their baby will be the first grandbaby, or give their baby a name that name that closely resembles our child's name. Trust me, someone will call their child by the name of our deceased child, and that hurts more than anything.

I have endured every aspect of this post. Especially the last parts, and it didn't have a happy ending. We don't ask for the world to stop, or for others to not be happy, but to some extent, we have earned the right - and that of our child's memory - to be respected. Just some food for thought; chew slowly. Love and hugs.

123

I've heard it said it's hard watching your child grow up so fast. Try never getting to see them grow up at all.

I have been blessed with a loving and handsome step-son whom I love very much. I have watched him grow from the age of ten to a wonderful man, aged twenty-two. I have been taken aback at how fast the time has flown by, watching him play baseball and go from the last years of elementary school to graduating from college. I can't imagine how my husband feels having been there since day one 'til now. But I have watched my step-son grow up over the past ten years, and it has flown by.

Sometimes I feel cheated when Makaylee's birthday comes around. I often feel cheated and left out of the joys of life because she died. I had prayed for her for so many years - to become pregnant. When I did, and then tragically lost her in a very traumatic way, I not only lost witnessing her birth, but I lost her growing up as well. A piece of me dies every single day, knowing that I have missed out on everything I ever dreamed of. Having to visit a headstone is not the way I envisioned being a mother. I would move Heaven and Earth to have my little girl back and to watch her grow into the beautiful woman I know she would have been.

Much love and hugs for a pleasant day.

124

When people cry, it's not because they are showing weakness or defeat; they cry because they have had to be so strong for a very long time.

Sometimes we just need to cry. I think a lot of people don't cry enough. The world we live in is never an easy, fair or forgiving place, and for those of us that have buried a child, the world can be downright unbearable and quite judgmental.

Struggling through life without ever losing a child is hard enough, but when you lose one, struggling becomes obsolete. Sometimes all you can do is cry. Cry for the broken dreams, for the happiness of becoming a parent and for all the things you had envisioned for the baby you were to have.

I know that I find myself shedding some tears often, and I have come to realize that even with time, the tears come more often. Sometimes, I think they are for wanting to be with my Makaylee, but in no way does breaking down mean that I'm weak and unable to move on.

Our tears show that we loved, and still love, our child. When you became pregnant, you became bonded together, and that connection can never be severed, not even by death.

So crying is not a sign of weakness, it's a sign of enormous strength that most people will never understand. Love and hugs, my friends.

125

Child loss is just not an event. It becomes an indescribable way of life, of just trying to survive.

By definition, an event is a "thing" that happens. When you lose a baby, it is definitely not an event. It is a life changing experience. Your heart and soul have started a new way of life, and the hardest part is surviving it.

Finding a path to cope with your loss is a never-ending journey that will have you on a roller coaster of uncertainty and heartache. By nature, when tragedy happens, we have a flight or fight response.

Depending on the situation, one or both responses kick in. When we bury a child, the fight to keep our sanity is what takes over. The overwhelming need to reject the thought that this horrible tragedy has happened to you utterly consumes you, and at some point in our grief, we just want our reality to be nothing but a nightmare.

That's the flight response. I often found myself trying to refuse to accept that the headstone with my daughter's name on it is truly my reality.

The emotions we experience on this journey are all part of the grieving process. It's a never-ending cycle that has no rhyme or reason.

There are no rules or guidelines on how to survive this all-terrain path that we've been put on. Just surviving can seem hopeless, but there is a silver lining. We have each other.

This group of understanding and loving parents that have all been walking this path of grief can now join hands with others, making child loss a little less lonely. Love and hugs, my friends.

126

When a butterfly happens to land on a flower near us, it's like having the sunlight warm our face, and for a brief time, the beauty is here for us to take in. But just as silent and quietly as they appeared, they leave just the same. And even though we wish it would have stayed longer, we are forever grateful that we were able to see it at all.

Butterflies are very beautiful and delicate, and just like our baby, they're here one minute and gone the next. Their silent existence is a reminder of how our lives were with them. One minute we were just an ordinary person, and then suddenly, they are quietly placed in our womb, just like when a butterfly lands on a flower.

And just like we gaze upon God's beautiful creation, we also recall seeing our little one for the first time on the ultrasound monitor. Nothing can ever compare to the beautiful perfection of our baby, but as the butterfly only stays for just a few fleeting moments, so too, did our little ones. *Too beautiful for Earth,* as I've heard it said.

And even though it pains us so much to see them go, we know that we will see them again, and we become so grateful that we even saw them in the first place. Love and hugs.

127

All we want is for our pain and grief to be validated. Not for it to be feared or shamed, and not for anyone to fix it, we just want it to be acknowledged and not forgotten.

A lot of times, I feel like we don't get the recognition and respect we deserve for the position we hold. Being a parent to a child in Heaven is, by far, the hardest thing most of us will ever have to endure. I know it has been mine. When our journey begins, family and friends tend to be more involved with helping us to cope. Sometimes, they are not so inclined to aide us in finding ways to learn our new way of life, and as time goes on and the months turn into years, the memory of our child tends to go unnoticed by those we would love to be there for us the most.

And that in itself can be very detrimental to our recovery. I know that the world doesn't revolve around those who have buried a child, but when family and friends don't show recognition in regards to the baby we had to let go, it just hurts even deeper. Acting like nothing happened, or saying that we should not still be grieving so hard for our child because they are not in the grave we sit and cry over but in Heaven, is not going to fix our heartache.

Trust me when I say that we've lost a child, not suddenly become ignorant. We know that they are no longer in the grave and that they are sitting with God, but telling that to our hearts is a very hard and delicate subject. We know that the world does not revolve around us or our grief. We don't want it to. We are not selfish in that way, but a kind, loving word or gesture of acknowledgment for the child we carried would mean the word to us.

That our tragedy did not go in vain. Your child will always be remembered here. Love and hugs, my friends, love and hugs.

128

See me as I am; this is me grieving. Yes, there are, and will be, many tears. Sometimes uncontrollable sobs followed by immense anger. Confusion will sometimes take hold of our thoughts, leading to forgetting the smallest of things. Some days I will smile, and a laugh will escape my closed lips, but always remember we have not forgotten our grief and never will.

Our grief can be overwhelming to others, especially if they have never had to experience it themselves. The death of a child can be very hard to understand, along with the grieving experience. I know I often find myself wiping tears from my face, whether it's from seeing a commercial showing newborns or just glancing around my house, feeling the emptiness of not having my child here with me.

Living life, Lord knows I have fallen to my knees in absolute surrender to the heart break I consistently feel each time I visit my daughter's final resting place, sobbing so hard that I can't find my breath or the will to want it. Rage consumes my heart when I see or hear about a child being mistreated or killed by the people who were meant to protect them.

Confusion on why this has happened to me, and someone who neglects their precious gift from God gets to have as many children as they can. Sometimes, forgetting that I'm still alive is the hardest reality to have to live with. Wanting to forget that my child was ripped away from me, I had prayed and felt deserving of the child that I was blessed with for twenty weeks.

Having to force a smile on my face to help make others not feel uncomfortable around me when I'm feeling so broken inside, laughing at things just to appease others, is very tiresome and difficult, especially when laughter is nowhere to be found. Never having a second from reliving my short time with my Makaylee and the bond we had formed but never got to experience and never forgetting any detail of my miraculous pregnancy and the way I fell in love so quickly. Always replaying the horrible reality of never being able to forget how broken I feel without her. It all adds up to an unbelievable amount of grief that will never leave my heart or my memory. But after all is said and done, my love for her lives on inside of me, and nothing or no one can ever take that away. Losing our child will forever be a constant, unwanted reminder that we've done the impossible; we've had to let go. And to me, that has been the hardest thing I've ever had to live through. Love and hugs.

129

During the times I am sad, I truly don't need for you to tell me it will get better, or that I need to find a way to move on. I just need you to tell me that everything will be okay, and that it is perfectly all right to be sad. I just need you to be open to my pain, and let me know I'm not alone. That I am strong, even when I'm at my weakest. That's all.

Why does it feel like the world has put a stigma on child loss? Why does it have to seem like nothing ever happened, as if a child never existed or departed from this world? People who have never watched a life leave this world have no idea what it does to the human soul. How it utterly consumes you, crushing your spirit and leaving a hole in the very center of your heart.

When I was a licensed practical nurse (LPN), I sat by many bedsides and held the hands of dying patients until they drew their last breath. And even though they were not kin to me, I treated them as such. I lost my daughter five years before I became a nurse, and I know that going through that tragedy helped me be a better caregiver. And while it's never easy to say goodbye to any loved one, having to say it to a life that never truly began totally changes you. The sadness consumes every fiber of your being, and absolutely nothing can make it go away.

Now just like anything else, we learn to survive in our sadness, but it's not, by any means, us moving forward, or us forgetting. We find ways to self-soothe, because no one, unless they've been through the same circumstances, knows the brokenness we carry around. Nor do they know how to help. Child loss needs to have that stigma removed and replaced with compassion. Love and hugs, always.

130

Just because I grieve, doesn't mean I have a contagious disease. I just miss my baby very much. I need to mourn at my own pace, because my entire life has been forever changed. Don't feel the need to share your opinion if you haven't experienced my pain, and please stop telling me to move on or get over it. These are not an option for me, and they wouldn't be for you, either. I'm doing the best I can by putting one foot in front of the other, even if it takes me the rest of my life.

When grieving becomes a normal way of life after child loss, the side effects seem to inconvenience others. I've often been treated differently because I have to plan my life around my grief, depression and anxiety. Large crowds seem to smother me, and that has been a big adjustment for me.

Before I lost my daughter, I had been a ballet dancer for fourteen years, marching commander of my pompom squad in high school, and was a part of Broadway play while I was in high school. I used to be very outgoing and loved to be in the spotlight, but death changes all that, especially when it's your own child.

I can recall a conversation I had with a coworker many years ago. He friend had lost a child, and I remember saying that I hoped that I would never have to experience such a tragic loss. Well, fourteen years later, here I am, living the words that flowed from my mouth so many years before. We all have learned the hard truth about life, and while we each have this in common, we each have a personal way of dealing with our pain.

Just move at your own pace. Don't let others influence you to rush through your loss. Just breathing can be an absolute challenge. I never leave my home without my medication, and I visit my counselor as often as I can. Anxiety plagues me so often that I have to bring my emergency medication with me everywhere.

I know it's hard to do, but don't hide from your grief. It's okay to own it and show it when necessary. Be bold, my friends. Love and hugs.

131

I already know that when I get to Heaven, the very first thing on my list is to find you and secondly, never ever let you go.

Oh, what a beautiful dream to look forward to. Holding our baby for the first time, getting to finally feel her skin and hug her and for her to hug me in return. It's an image that is forever burned in my heart. When I visit the graveside, I often find myself yearning to feel complete again, by wishing Makaylee would just appear from the woods surrounding the cemetery. We would run to each other, and I would wrap her up so tight.

Sometimes, I wish it to happen so badly that I have major anxiety in leaving. My friends, I know that it is extremely hard, and downright unbearable, to want something so badly that you know can't have until

God deems it so. But until that day comes, keep dreaming of how beautiful and wonderful our reunion will be. Much love and hugs.

132

When I started *Mothers of Angels,* I not only wanted to have a judgment-free place where parents who share the same sadness of child loss, I also wanted to help make a difference - in not only my survival, but possibly someone else's. I have suffered from panic attacks for many years. That it is literally a way of life for me.

I hate that I have absolutely no control over when - or where - my attacks happen. They are very unpredictable and very inconvenient. I've had blood work done showing that I have two abnormal genes that will always keep me in a cycle of anxiety and depression. As you can imagine, I was not excited to hear that kind of news. But with medication and counseling, I can try my best to stay ahead of the game.

Mine has gotten so bad through the years that I have to take medication at night, just so I don't wake up in a state of panic. That happens a lot. The death of my daughter was the trigger that started this roller coaster ride of living life second by second. Child loss forever changes you on levels you never knew you had, and you will never be the same person you were before this horrible tragedy.

But getting help in treating the anxiety that accompanies child loss can make a world of difference in your survival of it. I pray for each and every one of you, my friends. Love and hugs.

133

My sweet child, you are always the very first thought when someone tells me to make a wish.

At some point in life, we all are a little superstitious. Like wishing on a dandelion or making a wish when an eyelash falls out. I know a lot of people who knock on wood in hopes of maintaining an air of good vibes. I'm one of those, not that I think black cats, broken mirrors or walking under a ladder will bring you bad luck, but I do knock on wood. When you've almost died three times in your lifetime, I think that knocking on a little wood won't hurt.

Which brings me to making wishes - like the age-old tradition of making a silent wish before blowing out candles on your birthday cake. Oh, how I wish that this one was true. I find myself in the bargaining stage of grief a lot. If only I had something that God wanted more than my Makaylee, I would gladly, without hesitation, give it to him if it meant that I could have my baby back. I know a lot of you have had these feelings, too. It's just not talked about, because of the fear of being chastised for wanting something so bad that we would be willing to do just about anything to make it happen.

Wanting our baby back is, and always will be, the biggest wish we want for ourselves. So, if you find yourself day-dreaming of what could possibly be done to bring your baby back, don't feel bad. It's only natural for a mother to want her child and to protect those she already has. A little superstition never really hurt anyone - just like making a wish before blowing out the candles on a birthday cake never hurt in wishing our baby would be in our arms when we opened them again. Much love and hugs.

134

Things not to say to a mother in mourning:

- Maybe it was God's will.

- Your baby was so sick, maybe it was for the best.

- They aren't hurting anymore.

- You were only a few weeks along; you really didn't get to know them.

- There will always be time for more babies; have you thought about trying again?

I know each and every one of us has heard these remarks before. Lord knows I have. I've never been one to question God's will, and for many years, I never asked him, *why my child*. Why the one thing I ever wanted, and longed for, got taken away from me. Sure, I found myself angry with God, because I had wanted Makaylee more than anything else in this world. I can only assume that something might have happened to her if she had lived.

I was one week away from finding out if she had inherited my heart disease. God knew that I would have probably not been able to handle what my parents went through with me and all my surgeries. I know that I will never know, this side of Heaven, why Makaylee had to leave. But for those of us that had to lay to rest our hearts' desire, it's hard to hear that it was God's plan. For those of you who had to helplessly watch your child fade from this world because of sickness need not to be reminded of how healthy and better they are now that they are in God's hands.

The Bible tells us for everyone who is saved and trusts in the Lord, know that we all will be in a perfect body one day. For those of us who suffered an early miscarriage and not getting to know our precious baby, well, we did know our child.

We carried them and were one, for however long God chose for us to be together. So that's never been an issue. As for the statement of having other children, for most of us, this will never happen. For others, being blessed with other children is a beautiful, wonderful, second chance, and I know that other pregnancies after the loss of one will be treasured even more.

But for those of us who don't get that second chance, the memory of our child lives on in our hearts forever. And that's something that no one can ever take away from us. Love and hugs.

135

You can't just bury a child and not feel the deep and very painful scars that are left behind.

When all is said and done, the actual death and burial of our child affects us deeper than we realized. Once family and friends stop calling or coming by, the inner source of our loss ultimately consumes our every thought and feeling.

Smothering out any feelings of acceptance in regards to believing our baby is really gone. Motherhood will no longer be a reality for the child we carried within our womb.

There will never be a happy ending or piece of mind, because for us, time stands still. We are forever stuck, waiting for a baby that is never going to come, and everywhere we look, we are reminded of all these things and we proceed to digress. So in a way, we feel as if we have been buried alive, and no one can hear our screams of extreme grief and heartache. It's like being given a life sentence on death row, but every time we think we might have a small window of peace for our parole, life quickly reminds us that our time is not up yet. And while we never asked to be in this position, we have to live in a world that cruelly judges on matters they know nothing about.

All we can do is find others that have had to endure the same heart wrenching experience of child loss and stick together. *Mothers of Angels* is always here. Together, we can - and will -survive this prison sentence. Love and hugs.

136

It was my job, as your mother, to protect you at all costs. I was going to guide, instruct and love you all the days of your life. I never knew that I was going to mourn you for the rest of mine.

It's amazing the transformation our thinking becomes, when we find out we are expecting. While we take every precaution to keep ourselves healthy for our baby's development, we instinctively become very consumed with protecting our precious baby at any cost. We start planning on how we are going to raise our child and how to keep them safe once they are born. We spend the better part of our pregnancy thinking of ways to protect them in our home and from the evils of this world.

We also fall deeply in love with the tiny little bundle of joy we see thriving on the monitor and ultrasound pictures. With each passing day, our love grows deeper and deeper for the child we patiently wait to meet. But when God has other plans for our baby, and we have no control over what happens, everything we had planned out in our minds now belongs to him. We are left to grieve for everything that was to be, but will never happen. We feel like failures, because we couldn't protect our child from death's grip.

All the hopes and dreams we had, of teaching and guiding our child through their lives, have now become memories of what might have been. We never wanted, or asked to be, a parent who mourns their child for life. Crying over the tiny plot that memorializes our baby is not what we had envisioned for ourselves, but that's what we now have to endure.

Remembering them is our love for them, and taking care of - preserving - the trinkets and flowers for our baby's final resting place is our way of protecting them as any parent would. Love and hugs.

137

Never feel like you have to rush your healing. Never pretend to be all right when clearly you are not. and never apologize for being utterly broken.

Losing a baby is a loss so great that healing from it is not an easy process. No matter what you do, there will always be a piece missing from your heart, regardless of whether you have more children, or how many years go by. Nothing will ever heal that type of hurt. But for some of us, we will never get a second chance at motherhood. So, healing our broken heart will never happen. Some broken things can never be mended, for the days you feel the deepest sadness, you should never hide your feelings. Losing a child is not something you stop mourning over. If those around you cannot understand that, then that is their problem, not yours. Never apologize for breaking down.

Having to bury your child is not supposed to be a quick recovery. Scream when you need to scream, cry when you are sad, be angry as much as and however long you see fit. It's your right as a parent to an angel. Much love and big hugs.

138

Things I've Learned:

Never, not even for one second, should you feel guilty for feeling sad. Trust me, everyone mourns differently. You will never get over the loss of your child, because there are no time frames or rules saying you have to. When people force you to cope with your grief, that's a sign of their own weakness. It's not healthy to hold your pain all by yourself. Never underestimate my sadness for vulnerability - or a reason to hurt me further. Don't think my tears are a sign of weakness, for they carry more strength than any hurricane.

My bad days may out number my good days, but they are both equally important.

Having doubt in your beliefs is only a part of being human. Faith is believing, not necessarily seeing. When I visit my child's grave, make flower arrangements or look at pictures, it's not that I want you to feel sorry for me, I just want to remember that I'm still a mother.

Grief is truly a learning experience. Those of us that are living through child loss constantly have to evolve to what gets us through the day. All my life, I have used music. It seemed like there has always been a song written that explains my every thought and feeling I was experiencing at that time, never more so than after my daughter's death. I have a large collection of songs that make me feel close to my child, because the words sometimes say what I can't.

A lot of people think because I have known loss most of my life, that I would know how to manage each day since Makaylee died. But I'm here to tell you, child loss has, by far, been the hardest time of my life.

Even with counseling and the help of medication, I still struggle with depression and find myself fighting anxiety on a daily basis. Even my counselor says that grief is a never-ending learning experience. With help, we still have those days that we have to find something to help ease our pain and sorrow. I've been told that going to the cemetery as often as I do isn't healthy. But those who have no clue what kind of hurt we feel - and have to endure every day - haven't been truly touched by death's grip.

You can't tell me that if their child was very sick in the hospital, that they wouldn't be right at their bedside, providing reassurance and compassion to their frightened child. Well, just because our child is physically not here, doesn't mean that we don't worry about them. And when we visit their graveside; we are, in a way, showing our love and compassion for our child by keeping flowers on the headstone and the area around them clean. We may never find an easy way to get through our grief, because it will always be hard to handle. But we can be there for one another to lessen the burden. Much love and hugs, my dear friends.

139

You may have been born silent, ever so perfect and always beautiful. You will still be loved, missed and always remembered, every second of every day. You may have been stillborn, but you were still born.

I've always wondered what it would have felt like to have heard my sweet baby take her first breaths in this world. Getting to hear everyone in the delivery room tell me how beautiful she was and wishing me and her father congratulations. Getting to finally hold her for the first time, telling her it was nice to finally meet the little one who had been kicking and moving around inside my womb. Unwrapping her from her swaddling blanket to count her fingers and toes, feeling her soft skin against mine. Breathing her in and telling her how much I loved her, even from day one. That she truly was a living miracle and a testament of God's miracles.

Instead, I only have a few ultrasound pictures to leave me with my imagination to live out that dream. I know she didn't suffer, because my doctor reassured me that she died instantly when my uterus ruptured. To help me feel like my daughter's short life and death weren't in vain, my OB had a recognition of life certificate made for my daughter. That meant the world to me, in more ways than one. Most people would say she never lived since she never drew breath outside the womb, but she did live. She was born straight into God's loving arms, and that is how she is remembered in my heart. Stillborn *BUT* still born. Love and hugs, sweet friends.

140

Courage is not having the strength to go on; it's going on when you don't have the strength. -Theodore Roosevelt

A lot of people forget that it takes a tremendous amount of courage to get through something as traumatic as losing a baby. It's not just an emotional connection that we have to compete with, it is finding the knowledge of how to accept that our child is never coming back. For every emotion that some people experience every once and a while, we are thrust into a constant whirlwind of every single emotion ever imagined, hitting you from every direction, every second of every day. Mourning for our baby is a full-time job, and we don't get a vacation from the sadness we carry in our hearts. Our courage is deeper than most can ever fathom.

The fact that we can hurt so much all day and manage to find the strength to open our swollen eyes, red from the silent tears we cry at night, and deciding to get out of our beds where we feel safe, is in itself courage. We have been given the toughest burden to bear that will never get lighter to manage, and to me, we may seem weak to others, but my dear friends, we can move mountains with all the love and courage we have for our baby as we work tirelessly to preserve their memory. And that my friends, is something to be proud about. Love and hugs.

141

I found a picture that shows the grief and anguish that we feel every day. It's a woman gripping her pillow with such power that you can feel her pain, without her even saying a word.

Know that just because we are grieving the loss of our child doesn't mean that we are not happy when someone close to us announces their good news of expecting a baby. The truth is, it is extremely hard for us to not feel torn between sharing in your happiness and the heart break that the announcement is not our own. For some of us, that day will never come, and it is a very hard pill to swallow and keep down, hidden behind semi-sincere smiles and congratulations. Though try as we may, sometimes the pain is so overwhelming, and it leaves us calling out to God, *why not me*. Some people may feel that this is selfish and self-centered on our own loss, but let me just say, it's not easy to watch as others have something we have wanted for a very long time. And having to face the reality of our misfortune can leave us screaming for answers and comfort that will never come.

Love and much hugs during times like this, and hope that some peace comes over your broken spirit and damaged heart.

142

For tears can always be wiped away, but this pain in my heart will forever remain.

Heartaches are so hard to live with, especially when it involves the loss of a child. The word heartache sometimes really doesn't describe the depths of pain we feel when we lose a baby. To paint a better picture of what our pain feels like would be like trying to paint a Picasso. He had a very unique way of painting his feelings so that, unless you had experienced the same situation, you honestly could not see the true expression of his art. My thoughts are left in turmoil, as I can't always express the pain I feel when I think about my daughter. I do feel a lot of anguish when I see children who are mistreated or killed at the hands of those who were supposed to protect them, while I have to stare at a headstone. And while you can wipe away the painful tears of sadness, you can never rid yourself of the agony you feel from the depths of your heart when you have to say goodbye to your baby. Nothing - or no one - can ever make that feeling go away. God bless you all. Love and hugs.

143

"People have said, 'don't cry,' to other people for years, and all it has ever meant is, I'm too uncomfortable when you show your feelings. Don't cry. I'd rather have them say, go ahead and cry. I'm here to be with you." -Mr. Fred Rogers

Growing up, Mr. Rogers was a huge part of my television education. Not too long ago, my husband and I went to see *A Beautiful Day in the Neighborhood,* starring Tom Hanks. I highly recommend watching this movie. The reason why is because of the quote I posted above. For parents who have lost a child, it is very benefiting to our everyday lives. It also could be used in telling our loved ones how to manage - and be there for us - when we need them. Let's face it; the majority of people get very uncomfortable when it comes to knowing how to emotionally be there for us when we have a bad day.

And we know that we have more rough days than most, because the death of our child never subsides from our minds. We truly never get a break from our heartache, and yes, we do cry a lot. And when those times come, no matter how often, it's nice to know someone is there.

Not being judgmental, or quick to share their opinions, on how our grief should be less by now. Mr. Rogers said it perfectly by saying that everyone needs to be there for everyone for every reason. As parents to angels, it's all we can hope for each and every one of you. Tears are very much welcomed here, and in the famous words of our childhood neighbor; "I'm so glad we had this time together. I like you just the way you are." Love and hugs, my friends. I'm so glad we are neighbors in the *Mothers of Angels* neighborhood.

My husband and I went to the cemetery to change out the flower arrangements, and while Shane was getting the cleaning supplies from the trunk of my car, I did what I always do and said hello to my

Makaylee. My husband happened to capture this moment, and I decided to share it with you. Recently, we've had several people close to us reveal that they are expecting, and while we are happy for them, I still struggle with never being a mother again. Even though I love making unique arrangements for my baby, it's still extremely difficult for me to find happiness for others when all I have is this memorial with my sweet baby's name on it. I know to some people, that may sound childish and selfish, but those who share the same heartache I do will completely understand what I mean.

This picture, as my husband said, captures the raw truth of child loss. The level of pain we still feel, after years of our child being gone, never truly stops the little portion of hurt we feel when others announce their impending arrival. It's just a small part of the big, ugly reality of grief. It never gets easier, and our hearts will always hurt as those around us get to experience their new-found happiness. And we truly wish them the very best, but we will always find our grief waiting for us to have our moments of sadness - that we are not the ones making the happy announcement. Love and hugs, precious friends.

145

You may feel completely broken, but you are strong. Much can be said for how well you hold yourself together, especially when you feel like breaking down. This is part of your healing process. It will never be an easy journey and not always a pretty one. All that matters is that you just keep going.

Broken, such a powerful word just by itself, such an appropriate word to use when someone experiences the death of a child. I know I feel completely broken most of the time. Mourning can take a profound effect on one's entire being. But even through our brokenness, we manage to keep pushing forward, even when everything within us is screaming for us to just give up. My counselor has told me that I'm one of the strongest people she knows, because of my persistence to continue on, even when I feel like the world has smothered me out.

Makaylee's death has definitely been a true test, which I haven't always passed. It takes an extreme amount of courage and inner strength to withstand the blows we receive when our baby dies. How we continue to stand tall through ridicule, ugly comments and judgmental advice, we always manage to break through the darkness and prevail. And even when we have those moments of complete brokenness and people think we are showing our weakness, I think that we are really showing our strength at its finest. Not just anyone can carry the grief of burying a child like we do. Love and hugs.

146

Anyone who has grown mentally, physically and above all, spiritually, knows that true growth is not found in comfort.

Finding beauty in grief is a very, very hard thing to do. Having to physically let go of your child is, by far, the ugliest part of grief. But if you were to just think back to a time before their parting. Sure, life was hard, and there were some things we had to do that were not pleasant. But through it all, we managed. After losing a child, every aspect of your life is put through massive challenges, and all the things you thought were figured out prove not to be. Everything from our faith, our sanity and all around understanding of life is scrambled completely out of control.

And we are left feeling utterly abandoned by everything and everyone. We find ourselves looking endlessly for answers that will never come, and we try to find comfort in anything that will ease our pain. The sad truth is that life was never designed to always be beautiful and perfect. Comfort cannot make our baby come back, and it cannot erase the painful memories we have experienced throughout our lives. I have learned and come to realize that even through my grief, I have found some beauty in my heartbreak. It's all of you, my new friends, and the ability to help others with our stories. Comfort will never find its slumber within our hearts, because half of our hearts reside in Heaven with our baby, and the other half is constantly trying to keep our sanity. Much love and hugs.

147

While the sun will still rise in the east

And the shadows of darkness will fall at night

But nothing feels the same

And each day is not always bright;

All birds will still sing

While the flowers will still bloom,

Even though the beauty is breath taking;

It won't mean the same without you.

I'm so sad that you had to go;

It's caused me such pain;

Because you were so precious,

This world's loss is indeed Heaven's gain.

There are just some days that we wish the world would stop, for just a little while, so we can catch our breath and feel some peace, which we no longer know anything about. Since the death of my daughter, life has definitely closed the door on any peace from my thoughts. Some days, I do wish that the sun wouldn't rise or set, because it's just another reminder that I have lived another day without my little girl.

When the short life of my angel crosses my mind, even a beautiful sunny day seems to dim just a little. When I visit my darling girl at her final resting place, I hear the birds singing their sweet serenades, but I only wish that my baby could be here to see the beauty that unfolds all around me when I'm just near her. But I know she is in Heaven, where all these things are more beautiful and much sweeter to listen to. Even though we grieve our child every day, there are just some days that outweigh the others. For we know that had our child been given the chance at life, our days would have been more beautiful than anything we see, now that they are gone.

Heaven did gain a precious jewel the day our baby closed their eyes to this world and opened them in the arms of our Lord and Savior. While we remain on this Earth, we will never see the beauty of the days we wake up to, every day since our child died, but our love for them, and keeping their memory alive, can represent some small part of the beauty they left behind. Much love and hugs.

148

People say it's time to move on,

MOTHERS OF ANGELS

That I've mourned your death for far too long.

But what they don't know - it wasn't their child;

Don't sit and judge me behind your fake smile.

Losing your baby is like breath with no air;

One minute of happiness just turned into despair.

It's okay that you're not all right;

It takes unconditional love

To survive this heartbreaking plight.

You've buried your baby, a piece of you,

Letting go of future memories

To hold on to just a few.

Our tears are sometimes all we have

To keep us grounded and from going mad.

You see, what's been easy for most to achieve

Is something we've lost and will never be.

The tiny life that we cherished, beyond all else,

died before we could fully prepare ourselves.

So mourn as you wish,

there's no wrong or right way,

For our tears will continue to fall

Regardless, night or day.

And that's just fine.

Despite what others may think,

You've lost a piece of your heart,

Your missing link.

Grief has no time frame or expiration date;

If others can't understand this,

then walk away for your own sake.

It takes courage to live without your child,

So, mourn as you need to,

No matter how heavy or how mild.

Love and hugs, sweet friends.

149

Post-Traumatic Stress Disorder (PTSD) is a mental disorder that can develop after a person is exposed to a traumatic event. It's like being injured very badly and bleeding from it. Many times, we feel as if we are going crazy with flash backs and grief - that we sometimes feel shameful that we can't handle our emotions. But you wouldn't feel that same way for bleeding from a physical injury. There really are no differences between the two. It just shows that you are a survivor.

Losing a child is a very, very traumatic event, and losing an only child can be catastrophic. So much so that recovery from such a tragedy is virtually impossible. Even though I knew my pregnancy was not a safe one, and a small part of me knew that the reality of carrying my baby to seven months so she could be delivered by c-section was very slim. But just like any parent, I had hope and faith that whatever was to be, would be. This had been the plan since we found out my pregnancy was not a normal pregnancy. It was the safest option for both me and my unborn child. If I could carry her until seven months gestation, she would be far enough along to have a better chance of survival outside the womb, and cared for by the best pediatric specialists to aid her in the final stages of her development. And the risks that were so high for me to begin with would be monitored and controlled under strict medical care. The goal was for a healthy mom and a healthy baby.

So when my body gave out, just shy of sixty days from getting to meet my miracle baby, I suffered, both mentally and physically, deeper than most parents ever experience when they do get to raise their child. And try as you may, nothing can prepare you for the massive train wreck that is about to derail everything you've ever known.

PTSD is not just a soldier's disorder; it blankets over all of us who live through the unimaginable and endured the impossible. Watching an innocent life pass from this world, to enter into Heaven without getting to say goodbye, is the hardest thing I've ever done. I should know, my mother was still clinging to life when I found her after she shot herself. I was only five years old, but in a way, I do believe that I knew my mother was not going to be with me after that moment.

I was lucky, in a way, that this trauma erased almost every memory of my mother before that fateful day, because Lord knows my mental health would be more damaged than it already is. So when God chose to take half of my heart on October 26th, 2005, I just knew that my life would never be the same again. And just like a deep stab wound to the heart, I will never recover what I lost fourteen years ago. When something so traumatic happens for which there is no relief, we survive the best way we know how. And sometimes just surviving is the only thing that matters when living with PTSD. We can survive this together, my friends, because our angels would want us to. Much love and hugs.

150

My dear friends, there will be many days when you want to just give up. To throw in the towel and scream your way into Heaven, just so your mind may feel at peace.

The weight of our grief can become extremely heavy, and be so great, that it consumes every spare space we have in our hearts. And all we are left with is a painful surge of memories to which we hold dear with feeble hands.

Others cannot begin to understand the depths of our pain as we sit at the graveside of our child at every birthday, holiday or anniversary, wondering why this has happened to us.

We are left searching for answers to questions that plague our hearts and torment our every waking moment. And while everyone feels loss, there's none so great to live with than that of a child.

Wanting to give in to our brokenness is only natural, and we have every right to feel this way. For the innocence that was ripped away from us, without any warning, of the pain that would pursue our hearts in the wake of missing them.

But there is a small hope of peace in which we can rest our weary hearts, and that's with others who share our same sadness. The death of our child changes every corner of our hearts, and there are not many things that can ease our suffering - or mask our grief - than when we are reunited with our children.

But until God sends his angels to carry us home, we do the best we can to just survive. Even if it's too painful to breathe, we have friends here, through *Mothers of Angels,* that are more than willing to share some support. Much love and hugs.

151

It's okay to feel as if you are struggling. It's okay that you have to work at being all right. It's okay to fear for your future. It's okay if you have some bad habits or color outside the lines. It's okay if you feel absolutely exhausted and unwilling to let your grief go. It's okay to over-think things, or to ask why this has happened to you. It's okay to feel completely lost or confused. It's okay not to be okay.

It is extremely difficult to stay positive when you know you're missing out on so many things with the child you lost. Surviving the grief that accompanies burying a child is not just something you overcome; it's definitely a work in progress. There's no shame in being scared for your future, because losing your child clouds all the dreams you had for your life. We definitely miss the person we used to be. It's only natural to yearn for that carefree, somewhat naïve person we were. before the harsh reality of life slapped us in the face with the innocent death of our baby.

Coping with our loss comes in many different forms, and though something might not be the best way to handle our grief, we do the best we can. Everyone expects us to return to the same person we were prior to our loss, but sorry to disappoint everyone. We will never color inside the lines of our former life. It's just not going to happen, and that my friend is okay. Grieving takes a lot of energy, and most people will never understand that. Mourning utterly consumes every aspect of your life. It is a full-time job with no break for vacation. Missing your child is a natural emotion, and having to endure it 24/7, 365 days a year can leave you completely drained. Just know that you never have to get over the loss of your child.

If you find yourself over-thinking about the days leading up to your child's passing, it can leave you in a state of insanity. Just remember, it was completely out of your hands and fully in God's. One day, we will have every question answered and accept the reason why our child had to leave this Earth. I know I constantly struggle with the person I've become after Makaylee died. I often tell my counselor that I wish God would have taken me with her if he knew I was going to grieve as hard as I do. When I see parents who take their children for granted, or worse, I can't help but feel cheated, because I would have cherished my child.

Sometimes we find ourselves rushing through family functions, because of the pain that sometimes accompanies them. That's one thing family members struggle with the most, but it's because they don't understand it. This is part of our healing process in coping mechanisms. When we are told that our baby has died, the confusion of why this has happened to us never stops replaying over and over again in our minds and hearts. It leaves us very lost in a world that continues on, while we are permanently stuck in a world that no longer has our precious baby in it. That's a hard pill to swallow and definitely hard to accept as our new life.

We will never forget or move completely forward from the loss of our child, and that's something that others need to accept, not us. Love and hugs, dear friends.

152

WHAT WE FEEL. Anxiety can leave us feeling like we can't do certain things. Unable to function, too stressed to continue on. Feeling humiliated or physically incapable of doing anything. Always feeling on the verge of panic.

WHAT PEOPLE HEAR. You're not willing to try; you're overreacting or just being lazy. You need to get out there in society to help you cope with your anxiety.

For all of us, this list represents our broken, highly unpredictable lifestyle once we make it past the actual death of our child.

- When we say I am unable to do that, it refers to our inability to forget the memories that replay over and over in our hearts. And sometimes, it also means that we will never intentionally put ourselves in hurtful situations like baby showers, births or some family functions.
- Missing our child takes a lot from us, both mentally and physically. Mourning, as deep as we do, is a full-time job, and no, we don't always like our boss.
- Facing our own inner humiliation, because living with our grief is hard enough alone. But to have others involved, like our spouse or counselors, can be somewhat hard to face.
- Not being able to physically handle certain situations is a hard part of losing a child. When others want us to move on from our heartache, they expect us to do that mentally and emotionally. But we will never be able to do that.
- Panic attacks are a big part of our mourning. The mental anguish our hearts endure - on a daily basis - is extremely hard to muster through.
- And when we say; "I cannot do that," it means we can't do that. Don't force us to be someone different or to forget our precious baby that we will NEVER do, period.

The things that people hear sometimes show their ignorance to our feelings. We truly, from the depths of our hearts, want to be able to have a normal life again. But when we buried our child, all bets were taken off the table. We are definitely not shy in our grief. If anything, we boldly walk through fire, every single day, in order to preserve our child's memory. And I can promise that we *NEVER* over-react to anything when it comes to our child. If we want to buy trinkets and beautiful flowers in honor of our angel, then we will do so. Others would do the same if the tables were turned.

Lazy is not even in our vocabulary. If anything, we work harder than a lot of parents, because we have to fight the world - every second of every day - to maintain our hearts, and that, my friends, is not being lazy. When others get upset with us because we don't involve ourselves in certain situations, it just confirms that they have no idea what it is like to walk in our shoes. That the best way for us to heal is to sometimes just be separated from things that remind us of the precious gift we lost.

We never need anyone to push us into moving forward. Mourning our child is not a small situation that anyone can guide us through. Sometimes it's a walk we take alone, and please know that when we say, *NO, I DON'T WANT TO DO THAT, DON'T FORCE ME,* we mean it. And not in an ugly or disrespectful way, it's just that missing our child is something we never dreamed for our future. We didn't set out to be mourners, or have major anxiety at the drop of a hat. That's why *Mothers of Angels* was created. Love and hugs.

153

I'm unpredictable. I'm not always on time. I may not have everything together all the time, and you may find me sobbing often. Decisions are no longer of high importance to me, and I'm sometimes easily angered by reasons you will never fully comprehend. Well, neither can I. I am extremely lost, both in this world and within myself. Mirrors show nothing but a shell of who I used to be. This is true grief. Please be kind and patient, and love me through it.

I can recall just about every minute the full week I had to stay in the hospital after my traumatic miscarriage. In the darkness, staring up at the ceiling above my bed, I remember telling myself that I was not going to let the death of my child change my life. I didn't want to become just another statistic. But even though I kept telling myself this, everything within me was fighting a losing battle. In the blink of an eye, I morphed into this hollow shell of a woman that looked like me, yet not the same person I remembered seeing in the mirror prior to Makaylee's death.

Unreliable was - and still is - an understatement. The medication I take in order to help me cope with my loss also blocks out some of my short-term memory. And quite frankly, it's not always a bad thing, even though it can be quite frustrating. But without my medications, I would never have a chance at surviving my depression. I no longer make a lot of decisions, because frankly, my depression and anxiety keep me busy enough that my mind is constantly working overtime, just to stay ahead of the grieving process.

Sometimes people get upset with me because I don't go out a lot or seem to be angry at the world. Well, I am. Not necessarily at anybody I know, but I'm never completely happy, because my child, my only child died, and I was left behind to suffer the aftermath of her passing. Any parent would be angry if something happened to the child they raised and loved so very much, regardless of how young or old they were. A child's death will do that. It's an ugly realization, but it's the truth. The personality I used to have may make a small appearance every once and awhile, but it will never stay for long, because that part of me left with my child.

If other people could see the persons we've become, they would not like who they saw, either. And we never wanted to be this way. It's just the life we have been given, and this is how we have to live it. I am lost, and have been, since my heart finally realized that my Makaylee was never coming back. I doubt that I will ever accept that my child died, but I can manage through, the best ways I can find. Even if that means fake smiles to appease others, or keep them from feeling uncomfortable. Going to counseling twice a month, sometimes more, just so I can unburden my broken heart to someone who doesn't know me personally, just to keep family members from feeling obligated to comfort me.

This is what grief looks like. Yes, it is real and yes, it can be extremely ugly. But if we can just feel a small piece of love for who we are, it can make all the difference in the world. We just miss our child. Love and hugs, my friends.

154

The question that most people tend to stop asking after a certain period of time after a loss is, *how are you?* To most, it's just three words and nothing more. But to us, they mean everything. As grieving parents, we need to stop the stereotype of saying we are okay when we really are not. Believe it or not, these three little words help in our healing process.

Remember right after you buried your child, and people were so eager and concerned about our welfare? Now do you remember how long it took for those same people to stop asking this simple but very important question? I know I can. The concerns of family and friends seemed to stop within a month or so after we buried Makaylee. And when we were asked this question, it became few and far between. I also noticed that it became more of a robotic mannerism in which people felt obligated to ask, but felt very uncomfortable to hear the answer. Well, my friends, that time has long since passed. When the death of a child occurs, the main concern should be towards the parents, and not for just a short time, because the depression that takes root runs deep and just doesn't go away. And the sad part of this is that those who have endured the loss the hardest are the ones that need to be checked on often.

Grief consumes every available space in our lives, making it extremely hard to feel loved and supported by our loved ones. After all, it wasn't their baby. Now don't think of me as one sided on this subject. I know everybody in a family feels the loss and grieves in their own way, but the parents are the main ones who suffer the most. And we know that nobody can bring our baby back or take away our pain. But completely closing all communication regarding to our mental health after child loss can be a dangerous thing.

You either wind up shutting down all communication with family and friends, or worse, because all we want to know is that you miss our baby as much as we do, that's all. So no, we will not remain silent anymore about

the death of our child and how it has changed our lives.

We are *Mothers of Angels,* and we are stronger than most people will ever understand. Love and hugs.

155

Healing from child loss can be quite difficult. One day you may be feeling okay, when in an instant, the pain and sadness hits you like a ton of bricks. There is no time frame or process in the mourning state of mind. But just know that through it all, you will be just fine.

When your heart is completely crushed, shredded and torn apart by the death of your child, healing takes on a whole new meaning. Instead of weird, *complex and unpredictable* would make better sense. What other people don't see is how we hurt behind closed doors. We've actually taken on a form of multiple personality traits, figuratively speaking. We can put a smile on our face when we have to. We can act like everything is okay when it really isn't; we can do a lot of things that most people cannot. It can become very exhausting and frustrating. More than often, we always make sure that our heartache doesn't affect others, when we deserve just the opposite. I think our feelings should be considered more often, while those around us showed a little more human compassion and consideration.

It's not easy being someone you're not, when all you feel is complete and utter destruction inside. This way of life is guaranteed to be hard and full of sadness, because we have done the hardest thing ever asked of a parent. We had to come to terms with losing our child, and that's nothing anyone can just get over - or move on from. Our healing will never be finished, because the pieces of our broken hearts are the ones we can't get back. Much love and hugs.

156

"When she woke in the morning, the devil whispered ever so softly, 'You cannot face this storm.' With the look of a true warrior she replied, 'I am that storm.'" - Unknown

I feel that a lot of times we don't give ourselves enough credit or acknowledgement as to just how courageous we truly are. Every day, the world does everything in its power to discourage, shame or leave us to grieve by ourselves. Doing its best to make us feel weak and hopeless, because we miss our angel so much. But that's when we have to remember that *WE* are the warriors, not them. I know how hard it is to feel secure in our own minds, because the sorrow we harbor takes a toll on every aspect of our daily lives. Satan and the world see that as our weakness, and do their best to take us down even further. But little do they know, that while we look fragile and unsteady on the outside, on the inside we have the heart of a warrior. My friends, I know how difficult it is to wake up most mornings and face the day, and I also know the nightmares we have that constantly remind us that our child is gone. But even through all of this, we have managed to keep our heads held high - even if we have to prop them up sometimes.

It takes an extraordinary person to handle what we do every day. So yes, while the world stands in our face, screaming we will never withstand this storm, we can honestly look the world in its face and boldly say, *I am the storm.* Love and hugs from *Mothers of Angels.*

157

Always will I mention your name. After all, you deserve to be remembered, always.

When we talk openly about our angel baby, it's not that we want others to feel sorry for us or feel uncomfortable. Just because our child died doesn't mean that we are not proud of them. We still have the desire to uphold their memory by saying their name and sharing our stories of what little time we had with them. We are still proud parents, regardless of what others think. We are reminded every day that they are no longer with us. and we are fully aware of that fact. But sometimes it feels good - and therapeutic - to talk about their lives. We like to feel like their death, and our loss, was not completely in vain. For those around us, shutting our baby's memories out of their thoughts sometimes hurts us more than the actual loss itself. They wouldn't want their child to be forgotten. Just know, my friends; *Mothers of Angels* will always welcome your memories of your precious baby anytime, any day. Because here all babies are worth remembering. Much love and hugs.